FROM EVANGELICALISM TO PROGRESSIVISM
AT OBERLIN COLLEGE, 1866–1917

FROM *Evangelicalism to Progressivism*
AT OBERLIN COLLEGE, 1866–1917

BY JOHN BARNARD

THE OHIO STATE UNIVERSITY PRESS

# PREFACE

What is the purpose of a college? How should it serve society? What should it do for its students? These questions, frequently asked by Americans concerned with higher education, have been answered in many ways. A college, some have said, should stock the student's mind with knowledge and discipline the mental faculties. Or it should transmit to new generations a particular cultural heritage. Some colleges have sought to implant and perpetuate a religious faith. Others have devoted themselves to preparing students to make a living. Many have offered opportunity for social advancement, or been a place for forming friendships, or provided a convenient setting for the pursuit of pleasure. A few, Oberlin among them, have acquired a reputation for encouraging a point of view toward American life. The weakness of institutional restraints has permitted a variety of answers to be given to these questions, sometimes even within the same college or university.

In this study I have tried to identify and describe one strand in the complicated pattern of the history of an American college: the changing ways in which students at Oberlin thought about social issues between 1866 and 1917. This historical theme like any other has infinite ties with the larger life surrounding it. In pursuit of it, I have frequently found it necessary to discuss institutional, administrative, religious, and academic themes in Oberlin's history. However, I have confined those discussions to what seemed helpful in explaining the social outlook of students. There are, then, many events and episodes both important in Oberlin's history and interesting in themselves that are unmentioned here or only briefly touched upon.

I am indebted to Professor Richard J. Storr of York University, Toronto; Professors Robert H. Bremner and Mary E. Young of Ohio State University, and Professor David Burner of the State University of New York, Stony Brook, for reading the manuscript and offering many helpful suggestions. President Robert K. Carr kindly granted permission to use the records of Oberlin College. The librarians at Oberlin cheerfully made available the materials used in research. The Department of History of the University of Chicago and the Faculty Grants Committee of Oakland University provided fellowships and grants which greatly facilitated my work. I wish to acknowledge a special obligation to the late Professor Robert S. Fletcher who guided my first studies in American history and encouraged me to take an interest in the history of the College.

J. B.

*Cambridge, Massachusetts*
*March, 1968*

# CONTENTS

FROM EVANGELICALISM TO PROGRESSIVISM
AT OBERLIN COLLEGE, 1866–1917

## CHAPTER I

# THE EVANGELICAL COLLEGE

---

On a lowland, secluded site in Ohio's Western Reserve thirty miles southwest of Cleveland, two missionaries, the Reverend John Jay Shipherd and Philo Penfield Stewart, founded a colony and a college in 1833. The colony was to be a model of Christian piety for the people of the Old West, while the college would train young men and women for labor in that vast vineyard of the Lord. Each in its way would aid in the great task of spreading the Gospel message of salvation. Colony and college were named in commemoration of Jean Frédéric Oberlin, who had sacrificed worldly advantages and career in order to minister to the people of a barren, neglected part of Alsace.

In its early years, the Oberlin Collegiate Institute was similar to the other undernourished colleges so thickly planted in the West in the early nineteenth century.[1] A discouraging struggle for existence, a standard curriculum and rote methods of instruction, and a paternalistic cultivation of piety and character were common elements in their stories.[2] Oberlin, however, acquired some unusual features such as coeducation, a policy of admitting Negroes, an intense and constant support for abolitionism and other moral and social-reform causes, adherence to a mild form of Christian perfectionism, and the leadership of the powerful evangelist Charles Grandison Finney.[3] The College became famous for its advocacy of a variety of religious and reform causes, an association with the novel and the controversial that drew both support and hostility.[4] In the decade before the Civil War, however, two influences moderated the extremes of opinion and emotion with which it was beset. More northerners adopted the reform views associated with Oberlin, while the College curbed some of its idiosyncrasies and eliminated others. By the end of the war it more closely conformed to the academic, moral, and social patterns that prevailed at other American colleges. Faculty and students invested greater energy and resources in academic work. Still, if some of the peculiarities of the past had been subdued, a sensitivity to religious and social needs beyond the immediate world of the College remained as a legacy from its early days.[5] With considerable justification Oberlinians still looked upon the College as an institution of learning unique in the thoroughness and zeal of its application of evangelical ideas.

When James Harris Fairchild was elected to the presidency of Oberlin in 1866, a less intense evangelical tone began to develop. Finney, while he never relished the tasks of college administration, had been president since 1851. By 1866 he was determined to devote his entire energy to teaching theology and conducting revivals. Fairchild represented a current of the College's life which was both religiously and academically more conservative than that of his predecessor. The new president adhered to the evangelical mission inseparable from early Oberlin but with a suspicion of excessive religious enthusiasm. A long prior association with the College—his entire adult life was spent in its service—prepared him for the discharge of the responsibilities he now assumed. Shortly after his birth in 1817 near Stockbridge, Massachusetts, the family migrated to the village of Brownhelm, Ohio, only a few miles northwest of the future location of Oberlin. Fairchild received a conventional classical education in a local academy and the nearby Elyria High School. In 1834 he entered Oberlin with the second college class and continued with theological studies after the completion of the liberal arts curriculum. While studying theology he taught Latin and Greek to preparatory students, so beginning a career as teacher and officer which did not end until his death in 1902. Before his election to the presidency, Fairchild, like many teachers of the day, taught an array of subjects. Greek and Latin, mathematics and natural philosophy, theology and moral philosophy were all, at different times, under his charge. His instruction covered a substantial part of the curriculum of the old liberal arts college. By way of preparation, beyond undergraduate and theological studies, he briefly visited several eastern colleges.[6]

Fairchild had few of the qualities that made his two predecessors in office, Asa Mahan and Finney, striking public personages. They had been original, full of confidence, outspoken, and at times unpredictable. Fairchild impressed contemporaries with less dramatic, but perhaps equally useful, qualities: common sense, prudent judgment, modesty, kindliness, and generosity.[7] His modesty, which some called diffidence, showed in his account of Oberlin's history which he related with scarcely any reference to himself.[8] Doubtless he was one of the few college presidents, even in that bucolic age, who milked his own cow.[9] Although a pious and faithful minister of the Gospel, his religious temperament and convictions were not expressed through public soul-searching and confession in the way that had been common in Oberlin's early days. Unlike Finney, he never experienced a sudden, emotional religious conversion. As he explained in his later years, he was not subject to bouts of religious introspection because "being of a calm, sunny makeup, [I] didn't go through that."[10] Even after his death, according to his biographer, some old Oberlinians lamented that "he had never known the Pentecostal baptism of the Spirit!"[11] Fairchild had neither the talent nor the desire to preach stirring revival sermons as Finney had done and as many Oberlin residents expected the president to do. College and town revivals occurred frequently during his presidency, but he rarely preached the sermons that began and sustained them.[12]

Fairchild's formal theology was marked by a moderate evangelicalism.[13] In 1892 he published the lectures he had delivered to generations of theology students as *Elements of Theology, Natural and Revealed*.[14] In content his theology was largely a restatement of the evangelicalism of Finney. According to one student, "the same great principles" were maintained by both: freedom of the will, the simplicity of moral action, the moral nature of man, and reliance upon evangelistic methods for conversion. His theological reasoning, however, was less rigorous and his language less emphatic than Finney's. His "common sense" temperament manifested itself even in his formal theology.[15]

Fairchild believed the tried and simple evangelical formula of powerful preaching of the Gospel message of salvation was adequate to meet the religious needs of the day. In 1874, recognizing that millions of Americans were out of touch with evangelical Protestantism, he addressed the National Council of Congregational Churches on "The Character Essential to the Religion Which Shall Take a Strong Hold of the American People," reaffirming the saving might of the evangelical way.[16] The American people, he declared, needed "the Old Gospel in its simplicity and power, divested of the theological bewilderments which have gathered about it, and brought home to the soul with all its claims and motives and inspiration." His faith untouched by the theories of Darwin, Fairchild saw no need to harmonize religious beliefs and the findings of science. His published works reveal no trace of concern for the religious implications of the growth and refinement of scientific knowledge. Since he was untroubled by the new theories of evolutionary science and biblical source criticism, his only fear was that the spread of new doctrines might bewilder those in search of secure theological moorings.[17] His distaste for theological polemics was so strong that friends avoided even private discussion of issues in the troubled realm of science and religion.[18]

Seen in the light of Oberlin's history, Fairchild's views on the ends and means of collegiate education were as moderate as his religious doctrines. In his inaugural address, entitled "Educational Arrangements and College Life at Oberlin," he defended the College's past as he foretold its future.[19] In surveying the history of College and colony, he reaffirmed the determination of Oberlin's officers and faculty to encourage the development of an aggressive yet serving Christian spirit among the students. The Oberlin student did not withdraw from the world when he took up his studies. Religious and academic pietism formed no part of Oberlin's ideals. The student should be deeply engaged in the great moral concerns of his time.

> College life, with us, is not peculiar, occupied with its own exclusive interests, pursuing its own separate schemes, and governed by its own code of duty and of honor. Each student belongs still to the world. . . . The student still shares in the responsibilities of common life, and is here for the purpose of a better outfit for the work before him.[20]

The ideal student was both judge and activist, forcefully applying Christian moral principles to all human situations and institutions. A moral commitment, Fairchild believed, brought point and vigor to the acquisition of knowledge and the disciplining of the mind. As the universe was governed by a benevolent God, truth and goodness must ultimately be one, and true education should cultivate the knowledge, power, and will to effect great and godly ends.[21]

> The power comes from generous impulses and noble aims, a knowledge of men and a feeling of their wants, a knowledge of God and sympathy with his work. A human mind charged with learning but without any kindling of soul toward God or toward man, is not a power. The simplest heart that loves God and pities man is mightier far.[22]

Love, earnestness, and ready self-sacrifice, bolstered to be sure by a measure of learning, were sufficient human means of doing the Lord's work.

Fairchild's belief that education at Oberlin should directly serve evangelical Christianity never wavered. As he said in a Baccalaureate sermon in 1877, midway through his presidential term:

> Culture is found, not chiefly in the effort to train this or that faculty, or to develop each susceptibility for our own use and satisfaction, but in a life of self-forgetful service to God and to mankind. . . . Growth and strength of soul must come from grasping great realities out of one's self.[23]

After his retirement, in a long series of chats with Delavan L. Leonard, a clergyman interested in writing the history of the College, he said that Oberlin had always sought education and scholarship as means for its students, not as ends. Learning was necessary, but only "kindling of soul" would make learning useful to humanity. The student's character should be shaped so that he would "know how to work for humanity and have a disposition so to do."[24]

At the heart of this endeavor were the common interests of students and faculty and their trust in one another. Fairchild was greatly disturbed by the impending rupture of this bond as teachers devoted themselves to the advancement of knowledge. "Oberlin's danger is that in a day of specialists, narrow men will be chosen [for the faculty] and so character, manhood, womanhood and inspiring personal power will go. That would be a disastrous lapse from the Oberlin of former days."[25] If the teacher dwelt in a "purely scholastic world at a great distance from the student," his power for righteousness would inevitably lessen. Fairchild once advised a nephew who proposed to study several years in a German university in order to prepare for a career as a college Latin teacher to attend instead a theological seminary and then take a position in a western college. If he studied at a German university he might be able to "make books," but he would not be able to teach with "contagious enthusiasm."[26]

Oberlin's educational plan was designed to produce the self-sacrificing Christian. In theory and substantially in practice, Fairchild claimed, the Oberlin graduate was the result of a confluence of carefully channeled religious and educational forces. The intimate association of the College and the community, supporting each other in evangelical endeavors, was a major influence on the lives of undergraduates. Coeducation, with the personal restraints it required and its supposed similarity to life beyond the campus, was an invaluable ingredient in the Oberlin mixture. The preparatory department and the theological seminary made their contributions and extended the influence of Oberlin.[27] The welcome given to Negro students testified to a determination to practice as well as proclaim Christian brotherhood. The faculty was the mainspring of this intricate mechanism of principles and methods. It must not sacrifice ends to means in succumbing to new academic fashions. As Fairchild warned: "If the teachers and officers of the school should lose their warm interest in the great Gospel enterprises of our time, and should become occupied with their studies and calling simply as intellectual pursuits, rather than as involving the higher interest of men and of the kingdom of God, the character of the work would be greatly changed."[28] Finally the students, the object of so much attention from others, also helped to shape the institution. Oberlin, Fairchild claimed, had attracted generations of sober, dedicated students whose example daily inspired their descendants. These fine traditions had to be Oberlin's main reliance in the future. The precious fabric of "associations and impulses . . . [were] a rich heritage more valuable to our school than endowment funds."[29]

Fairchild's views on the relation between religion and education did not change during his presidency. Since ante bellum days barrages of criticism had been directed against the old college. Although Fairchild's years in office coincided with a creative period in higher education, he was little influenced by the reforms proposed and instituted elsewhere. The introduction of the elective principle, the broadening of studies to include modern sciences and languages, the maturing of professional education, and the appearance of the modern university with its methods of objective scholarship indicated a new mood and new expectations in the world of learning.[30] The old college at Oberlin and elsewhere had to reject outright, or accept in whole or in part many novel proposals. Fairchild did not stand adamantly against the new but he distrusted innovation and feared its implications. He was tolerant of change when it came through those who had the right to debate issues and share in decisions. His acceptance of the principle of faculty control of policy, with the president only a leading member of the faculty, made it possible to reconsider fundamental positions without debilitating friction.[31] Pressures for new departures arose and were expressed through the students, faculty, alumni, and board of trustees. Some of the changes made late in his presidency probably disturbed Fairchild, but he made no attempt to block them once the faculty had made its decision.

Fairchild was a leader of solid qualities who contributed to Oberlin's progress in many ways. With his firm, if narrow, moral and religious convictions, he exemplified his own ethical postulate of benevolence. His great modesty had led some to fear that he would not be an effective leader, but he enjoyed the confidence of the faculty and trustees. He did not relish the discharge of some presidential duties, such as soliciting funds and representing the College before large, unfamiliar audiences. During his regime these tasks were left to others. Despite Fairchild's inactivity in the sphere of solicitation, the College was in a relatively prosperous condition during most of the years of his presidency.[32] His intellectual and religious equipment, derived from a limited set of experiences and the evangelical ardor of an earlier age, prevented his complete appreciation of the new religious, educational, and social movements of the time.[33] As the years passed during his long presidency, he lost touch with the unsettling ideas that were increasingly agitating the minds of some Oberlin students and a few of his faculty colleagues.

The public reputation of Oberlin prospered under Fairchild. His biographer credits his "reasonableness and breadth of thought" with dispelling old misconceptions of Oberlin and animosities towards it.[34] Through mutual concessions the old differences with some Congregationalist churches over the use of evangelistic methods and the doctrine of perfectionism—the possibility of a sinless existence for the converted—both of which dated from the days of Mahan and Finney, were eliminated.[35] Oberlin could no longer be charged with heresy.

The College remained informally tied to Congregationalism through the affiliation of its leading figures, but, like other colleges founded by members of that church, it was legally independent since the nature of its organization precluded formal control. The founders, Shipherd and Stewart, were Congregationalists although Shipherd, working through the Plan of Union that united Presbyterians and Congregationalists in western missionary endeavors, had ministered to a Presbyterian mission church in Elyria, Ohio, before founding Oberlin. While the absence of formal denominational control deprived the College of one source of financial support, although many individual congregations did send contributions, it simplified the creation of a broader foundation when that became desirable in the late nineteenth century.

The composition of the board of trustees reveals the constituency that Fairchild's college aimed to attract and serve. At Oberlin the trustees have acted a lesser part than in most American colleges. The management of academic affairs, broadly construed, is in the hands of the faculty and president. Finney, whose sensitivity to trustee interference in academic matters was aroused by an incident at Lane Seminary in Cincinnati where the trustees forbade students to discuss emancipation of the slaves, insisted on this arrangement. He conditioned his acceptance of a position at Oberlin upon acquiescence by the trustees in faculty control.[36] The Oberlin board in 1866 when Fairchild was inaugurated had twelve members. It was self-perpetuating. Most of the members resided nearby: five lived in Oberlin, two in Cleveland, and two more in other Ohio cities.[37] Only three of the trustees were college graduates, although several others had received some college training. John Keep, elected to the board in 1834, had compiled the longest record of service. He failed of being a charter member by only a few months. The occupations of the board members were nicely balanced with five clergymen, five businessmen, one lawyer, and one doctor. Although business and professional men composed a majority of the board membership, successful business experience and professional reputation were not the most important criteria in their selection. The laymen were more noted for their support of religious and reform causes than for business or professional activities. For example, Francis Parish, a lawyer of Sandusky, Ohio, was an active churchman and a leading member of several Congregational and reform organizations. Samuel D. Porter, a businessman of Rochester, New York, had been converted by Finney and was a well-known friend of the Negro. Brewster Pelton, an early merchant and innkeeper in Oberlin, was known there for his support of Asa Mahan, Finney's predecessor as president of the College, who was remembered for his advocacy of Christian perfectionism. The historic commitments to evangelicalism and the moral and social reform causes of the ante bellum era were evident in the interests, reputations, and activities of the trustees.

Faculty members too were chosen in large part for their loyalty to evangelical religion and moral reform, a loyalty assured by drawing them almost entirely from the ranks of Oberlin graduates. In 1866 nine instructors taught the undergraduates of the Classical or standard four-year course.[38] All except two of these teachers, James Dascomb and James A. Thome, had earned a Bachelor of Arts degree. Dascomb held a medical degree from Dartmouth College and Thome had graduated from the Oberlin theological seminary. Five of the seven remaining faculty members had received their undergraduate degrees from Oberlin, and three of these were graduates of the seminary as well.[39] The remaining two professors, Charles H. Churchill and Judson Smith, had studied in the Oberlin theological seminary.[40] Every teacher in 1866, therefore, with the exception of James Dascomb, the only member of the original Oberlin faculty still teaching undergraduates, had received some part of his education at Oberlin, while a majority had received all of their academic training there.

In the view of Oberlin officials the hiring of alumni for faculty places was favored by both logic and expediency. In order for the College to convey effectively a fixed body of academic and religious truth, its teachers had to be wholly committed to the cause. Since the truth in matters of fundamental importance was fully known, the exposure of students to conflicting views or to a systematic search for truth was merely exposure to confusion and possible error. Such an argument, common at the old colleges, was especially persuasive at Oberlin.[41] Alumni, trustees, faculty, and students usually thought of the College and its ways and traditions as different, and most were proud of this distinctiveness. The most effective way to safeguard and perpetuate these hallowed characteristics was through careful selection of the faculty. Fairchild always believed that most of the faculty members should be alumni. It became, however, more and more difficult to find candidates who combined loyalty to Oberlin's evangelical tradition with respectable preparation for teaching. Fairchild proposed in 1887 the establishment of fellowships to enable Oberlin graduates to secure specialized university training with the expectation that they would later join the Oberlin faculty. Two such fellowships were soon endowed by the board of trustees.

That the services of alumni could often be obtained at minimum cost was a second strong argument in their favor. Since the College was frequently in financial straits, the use of graduates for teaching at low rates of pay may indeed have enabled it to survive.[42] The loyal graduate could often be induced to make a financial sacrifice for the sake of the College, a motive often referred to and praised in trying times.[43]

John Millott Ellis, a leading professor from 1858 to 1894, exemplified the desired qualities of the Oberlin teacher during Fairchild's presidency. A graduate of the College and the seminary, he successively taught Greek, rhetoric, mental philosophy, and moral philosophy. In many ways he stood for the loyalties of an older Oberlin that would soon begin to slip away. He was an ordained Congregationalist minister and a powerful spokesman for evangelical orthodoxy. He delivered innumerable sermons and lectures to undergraduates on current religious issues. For example, speaking in 1881 on science and religion, he condemned those who questioned the Bible as a direct revelation of God's will and who refused to believe in miracles or the efficacy of prayer. "The man who says that a miracle is impossible, makes the existence of God an impossibility, and to deny that prayer can be answered is to deny that there is any relation of creature and Creator." Such skepticism was tantamount to atheism, "and atheism is not only intellectual stupidity but moral folly." [44] Ellis frequently preached at the Second Church in Oberlin, of which he was a member, and in the churches of nearby communities. After one of his sermons a colleague wrote: "Prof. Ellis preached the best revival sermon I have heard since Mr. Finney's time on 'The Day of Visitation.' "[45] One could not receive a higher mark. Ellis was a dedicated moral reformer, an abolitionist and prohibitionist, and, like nearly everyone else in Oberlin, a firm Republican.[46]

His talents and principles made him an excellent representative of the College. He met often with alumni groups to speak on Oberlin and to solicit funds, thus relieving the president of that burden. Many older alumni saw in him a later incarnation of the revered ante bellum teacher, reformer, and evangelist. He defended propositions and qualities that were thought by many to be Oberlin's unique possession. At Commencement in 1865 he spoke on "Oberlin and the American Conflict," vindicating the part Oberlin played in the agitation of abolitionist views.[47] In the later years of Fairchild's presidency Ellis was the leading public defender of the old college. The many small country colleges, like Oberlin, he argued, had not wasted the nation's academic resources. By providing an opportunity for intimacy between teacher and student, by making college training available to many more students than would otherwise have been the case, and by tapping sources of funds unavailable to the large college or university, they had returned substantial dividends on the total academic investment.[48] Ellis fulfilled in another respect the hopes of the founders. They had believed that the success of the institution would depend in part upon harmony and mutual support between College and colony. Through community and college life an environment for the nurture of Christian character could be created. As town mayor, local preacher, leader of the Arboricultural Association, and prohibition activist, Ellis served both College and community.

He was regarded as an excellent teacher. Most of his instruction was in the old courses in mental and moral philosophy, then considered the keystone of college education. He was gentlemanly and courteous in the classroom, always willing to entertain questions and arguments from skeptical students.[49] When Fairchild resigned in 1889, he hoped that Ellis, although fifty-eight years of age, would be chosen as his successor. With a strong hold on the affections of many Oberlinians, Ellis received impressive support. Many alumni and faculty saw in him the means—perhaps the last hope—of keeping Oberlin true to familiar ways. Owing to his age, however, or to a desire for a president more congenial to change, he was not selected.[50]

A second prominent teacher of Fairchild's time was Professor Charles Henry Churchill, a native of Vermont, who had graduated from Dartmouth College in 1845. Soon after his graduation he moved to Ohio, taught school for a time in Cleveland, and then entered the Oberlin seminary. Like many theologues he helped meet his expenses by teaching preparatory students. During one term he received 18¾ cents an hour for teaching "Geography of the Heavens," as astronomy was then called at Oberlin. After his appointment in 1858 as professor of mathematics and natural philosophy, he taught mathematics, physics, and astronomy until his retirement in 1897.[51]

Churchill represents the teacher who chiefly served his students as a model of character, a common type in the old American college and considered indispensable. His personality apparently left a deeper impress than his instruction. A fellow teacher later wrote that Churchill was the "most beloved member of the Faculty" of his time, and many students felt a deep affection for him due only in part to his reputation as an easy marker.[52] He entertained students with demonstrations of physical principles on makeshift equipment, most of which he had contrived.[53] In addition, however, he secured for Oberlin its first professional apparatus for use in the study of physics and astronomy.[54] An unusually talented student, Robert A. Millikan, judged Professor Churchill's course in physics a "complete loss."[55] Another graduate wrote:

> Incidentally . . . I got least [from the Physics Department] while in College twenty-odd years ago. This was the result of the times fully as much as it was of the College, or of President [sic] Churchill. I should add that while I acquired little physics under him I did get many valuable lessons in kindliness, courtesy, and what is sometimes called sweetness of character, which after all may have been worth more than a little more physics.[56]

Churchill deviated slightly but significantly from prevailing Oberlin religious belief and practice. Although a seminary graduate he was not ordained and apparently never intended to preach. According to his son, he did not question the fundamental tenets of Christianity but he thought character more important than creed and he accepted scientific knowledge that was incompatible with a literal understanding of biblical accounts.[57] Having bought a copy of *The Origin of Species* as soon as it was available, he defended Darwin to a

Scripture-quoting friend, saying simply, "so much the worse for Scripture."[58] He read secular literature on the Sabbath, a practice that old-fashioned Oberlin piety did not approve, and he even took walks on the holy day when no one else on the faculty dared to do so "except two young men who had studied in Germany." Unlike many of his colleagues he refused to boycott a druggist suspected of selling liquor or a bookseller who refused to close his store on prayer-meeting evenings.[59] He was one of the few faculty critics of the custom of hiring Oberlin graduates for faculty places. It had led, he believed, to an unhealthy narrowness of view and to a decline in the quality of debate on important issues.[60] In addition, he favored the awarding of prizes to students for academic distinction whereas the great majority of the faculty strongly opposed such "artificial" incentives to good work.[61] Churchill's opinions illustrate the limits of variation within the Oberlin community during the early years of Fairchild's presidency.

Not all the faculty members of that time exactly fit the mold of Ellis or Churchill.[62] Yet, with only minor differences, they were remarkably similar in experience, character, and conviction. Like the founders of Oberlin, they sprang from families of rural or small-town New England origin that had migrated westward in the first half of the nineteenth century. In their religious beliefs and educational ideas they were more conservative than most of the descendants of the Puritans who remained in New England to guide the churches and colleges there. In 1880 Joseph Cook, the popular Boston orator, declared that Oberlin represented the original spirit of New England Puritanism better than any other institution.[63] In relative isolation from the economic, social, and cultural forces that were moving the New England religious and educational establishment toward acceptance of religious variety and new learning, Oberlin was still substantially loyal to its old ideals. By modern standards the teachers of Fairchild's time were superficially trained and, as a group, were too homogeneous to excite much intellectual vitality, controversy, and interest. For them and for many of their contemporaries, however, their inadequacies in formal training were of little importance compared to the moral and religious ideals for which they stood. Their restricted experience and intense concentration upon a limited range of issues tended to maintain their innocence, but in their judgment this sharpened the moral and intellectual weapons with which they attacked worldliness. Their efforts in behalf of evangelical Protestantism would contribute far more to the glory of God and the salvation of the world than any other task they might undertake.

The students who read, recited, and prayed under the benevolent guidance of the faculty were, like their mentors, less varied than their counterparts of today.[64] The Class of 1875, later noted for the accomplishments of some of its members, was typical of those of Fairchild's time. It included thirty-six members—thirty-five men and one woman—of whom thirty-five received Bachelor of Arts degrees and one received the Bachelor of Science degree.[65] Eighteen members of the class, exactly half, had been born in Ohio, and most of the rest came from other midwestern states. A few from eastern and southern states and two from abroad (one from Ireland and one of a missionary family from Siam) completed the class. Though the geographical distribution of Oberlin students in 1875 was narrow compared with twentieth-century classes, it was probably broader than in most other colleges of the time, thanks, in large part, to the national reputation of Oberlin for piety and reform.

The great majority of the class members came from farm and ministerial families. Seventeen were the children of farmers, eleven of ministers, five of businessmen, two of physicians, and one listed his father's occupation as that of cabinetmaker.[66] Home, for most of these Oberlin students, was either a middle western farm or town where their fathers were local ministers. With the important exception of seven clergymen's sons who intended to study theology, few of the graduates chose to follow in the footsteps of their fathers.[67] In 1882, when all were presumably settled in their work, it was reported that nine were teachers, nine were either preaching or preparing for the ministry, seven were lawyers, four were physicians, two were in journalism, two were in business, one had become an artist, and one was a farmer.[68] A college education had served as a road to the various professions, with the ministry almost replacing itself in the new generation. Its continued popularity attests to the hold on students of the most conventional form of evangelical dedication. Compared with students at most other colleges, Oberlin graduates found the ministry attractive.[69]

In the political opinions and affiliations of the graduates there was even less variety than in their occupations. The party of abolitionist idealism nearly monopolized political loyalty, with only a slight admixture of mugwumpery. By their own classification, twenty-nine liked their Republicanism straight, five were independent Republicans, one a Liberal Republican, and one an independent. The Democracy had no adherents in this Oberlin class.[70] Although that party usually had some support among Oberlin students, the proportion of Republicans to Democrats at Oberlin was commonly believed to be greater than in any other college.[71] On current political issues there was a large measure of agreement. The commitment to a reconstructed South was evident in the support given the Republican Party. On the international trade question, twenty-three were free traders, the high number reflecting perhaps rural origins and academic instruction in classical economics, three advocated a tariff for revenue only, and nine were protectionists. There was a far greater uniformity of opinion on the currency issue. Thirty-five reported that they favored a paper currency backed by specie, while only one was a "Pendletonian," that is, an advocate of an unbacked paper currency. Debtor radicalism had no appeal.[72]

Like other western colleges Oberlin tried to keep the costs of instruction as low as possible. College officials took great pride in the fact that at Oberlin an education was less expensive than at most comparable colleges.[73] Low costs were as much a traditional feature of Oberlin as its piety. Before the Civil War compulsory manual labor for all students had been tried as a way of reducing expenses, providing a means of student self-support, and affording a healthy relief from the cares and anxieties of study. This experiment, however, proved unsuccessful and was abandoned.[74] The College was often praised for giving poor but industrious youth an opportunity to gain an education. Indeed, one argument advanced against attempting imitation of the academic and social practices of eastern colleges was that it would require higher fees, creating an inhospitable social environment for the impecunious student.[75] Commencement festivities were censured as they became more elaborate and expensive, threatening to open a gap between the rich and the poor students that would undermine those solid principles of the founders, "pure faith, honest work and simple tastes."[76] Piety, integrity, industry, and a frugal, unostentatious mode of life were closely linked in the Oberlin scheme of values. The Class of 1876 reported an average expenditure of $1,300 for the entire college course, ranging from a low of $900 to a high of $2,100.[77] It was claimed, by way of comparison, that $4,400 was required for the education of a student at Yale College.[78] As late as 1885, College officials held that as little as $100, "added to the earnings of one or two hours' work a day—can be made to meet all absolutely necessary expenses for tuition, incidentals, board, room, fuel, lights and washing for a college year." [79]

In the Fairchild era, students were encouraged to work part time while in school as well as during vacations in order to meet expenses. Still the proportion of self-supporting students slowly declined. One observer claimed that the students who were supported by their parents were "less serious in character and outlook" than the earlier generations of self-supporting students.[80] In 1875 an investigation disclosed that 26 per cent of the students in the Classical Course were entirely self-supporting, 21 per cent provided one-half of the amount needed for their expenses, 19 per cent provided one-fourth, and 33⅓ per cent were entirely supported by someone else.[81] This investigation was undertaken as part of a debate on changing the "Long Vacation" from winter to summer. A long vacation in the winter aided self-supporting students by enabling them to teach in country schools. A vacation in the summer, on the other hand, had educational advantages. The board in 1877 adopted a new academic calendar with a summer vacation.[82] The College was not, of course, abandoning the self-supporting student by this decision. A statement in the *Catalogue of Oberlin College* encouraged part-time work and declared that "the traditions of the College, and the public sentiment of the students, favor economy in all living expenses." [83]

The curriculum of the Classical course during the early years of Fairchild's presidency was the standard western American college mixture of secondary and college subjects, covering roughly the last two years of present college preparatory work and the first two years of college studies. It had not materially changed since the founding of the College. The course either lacked entirely or treated only in a summary fashion many subjects now thought necessary for a liberal education. For admission to the freshman class one had to demonstrate proficiency in:

the common English Branches; the Grammar of the Latin and Greek Languages; Caesar, one Book; Sallust's Cataline; four of Cicero's Select Orations; Vergil's Aeneid, five Books; Harkness' Latin Prose Composition, Parts First and Second; Xenophon's Anabasis, three Books; Homer's Iliad, two Books; Olney's School Algebra or an equivalent; Olney's Plane Geometry; Ancient History; English Analysis; History of the United States; and Allen's Science of Government.[84]

The curriculum contained large amounts of Greek, Latin, mathematics, and religiously oriented philosophy with a smattering of science. Although studies varied somewhat from time to time depending on the availability of teachers, the four-year course followed this pattern:

*Freshman Year*
    Livy, Horace, and Cicero
    Xenophon and Herodotus
    Greek Prose Composition
    Mathematics including Algebra and Plane and Solid Geometry

*Sophomore Year*
    Cicero and Tacitus
    Homer and Greek Tragedy
    Geometry and Calculus
    Natural Philosophy and Botany
    Evidences of Christianity
    Rhetoric
    German and French

*Junior Year*
    Juvenal, Plautus, and Tacitus
    Demosthenes
    Astronomy, Chemistry, and Zoology
    Logic
    Modern History
    System of [Religious] Doctrines

*Senior Year*

Plato
Mineralogy, Physiology, and Geology
Mental Philosophy and Moral Philosophy
English Literature
Political Economy
Lectures on Art [85]

This was the plan of study until the mid-seventies when a very limited range of electives was introduced.

The formal curriculum was fortunately not the only avenue to learning. Its inadequacy was clearly demonstrated by the students themselves, who voluntarily undertook demanding and rewarding academic work outside the classroom. The most important extra-curricular agencies of education were the student literary societies, three for men and two for women. They provided an invaluable supplement to the narrow and unimaginative curriculum. In the second half of the nineteenth century, when literary societies on many campuses were falling victim to the spread of fraternities and the expansion of the curriculum, they thrived at Oberlin. Fraternities were not established there for several reasons: an old hostility to all secret societies stemming from Finney's antimasonry crusades and writings; the need to protect the system of religious aspiration and practice, which might be jeopardized by the rival loyalties generated by secret societies; and student devotion to purity and piety, which led to censure of fraternities for encouraging "gluttony, drunkenness, and ruffianism." [86]

The society exercises covered many subjects that were either inadequately studied in courses or entirely ignored. The staples of society work were literary topics, current public issues, religious and philosophical questions, and interpretations of notable persons and historical events. The program of the Alpha Zeta society on April 10, 1874, resembled hundreds of others. It began with a prepared critique of the essays, orations, and debate of the previous meeting. Such critiques were necessary to maintain high standards of performance. Then a student read an essay on "Agassiz," followed by an oration on "Stability and Progress," then another essay, this time on the puzzling subject of "Snow Power," and a final oration on "Aiming and Hitting." The meeting closed with a debate on the timely question: "Ought the Civil Rights Bill to Become a Law?"[87] The debates were thrown open to all members of the society after the assigned debaters had made their speeches, then a vote was taken on the merits of the debaters and a second vote on the merits of the question.

The Union Exhibition in May, when the best orators from each society spoke in public, was the high point of the year for the men's societies and an important College event. The preparations for the Union Exhibition of 1874 were described in this way:

> . . . strange sounds might have been heard at any time of day, and sometimes far into the evening, issuing from any of the groves in the vicinity. Every available stump was pre-empted, and the attention of quietly grazing herds was arrested by the score of orators in training for those grand occasions. All the churches, halls, and garrets were made to echo with the germinating eloquence, which afterwards blossomed and called forth such enthusiastic admiration.[88]

Since it was thought improper for women to appear in a contest before a mixed audience, the women's societies had their own union meeting from which the public was excluded.

Society membership was open to all save freshmen; upperclass students belonged almost without exception. The work was taken seriously. Fines were imposed for absence or tardiness. Failure to present an exercise when assigned was almost unheard of. In 1877 one society claimed to have had no failures for eleven years.[89] Many alumni testified to the value of society work. It provided excellent training in reasoning and in public speaking before a critical audience, gave students an opportunity to learn something of subjects which fell outside their formal studies, and forced them to resort to something besides teachers and textbooks for information and ideas. A large part of the worth of an Oberlin education resulted from the vitality of the literary societies. And, perhaps not least important, the societies encouraged student friendship and association.

The literary societies performed other important services for student intellectual and social life. Each society collected books for the use of members in the preparation of exercises. In 1874 they pooled their holdings in the Union Library Association.[90] The Association's collection, purchased with student dues, grew much more rapidly for many years than the college library and it provided an important supplement to the College's meager holdings in literature, history, and philosophy. The Association also founded and managed the *Oberlin Review,* the student newspaper. Some of the Association's funds were raised through a lecture series. These lectures often contributed to the intellectual life of the community and always to its social life. The College's great debt to the societies is indicated by the extent to which it now provides for students so many of the academic and social services once offered by them.

The curriculum and the literary societies were the means of intellectual training. The founders and President Fairchild contended that intellectual training was properly subordinate to the greater end of evangelical spirituality. Oberlin and strict piety were nearly synonymous. Great amounts of thought and energy were invested in the contrivance of effective means of encouraging conversion and religious dedication. In part the College relied upon a complex code of social regulations for undergraduates. All early American colleges had rigid codes of student behavior, but toward the end of the nineteenth century the original conditions and justifications for strict regulation of social life—such as wholehearted piety, the youthfulness of college students, and frontier conditions—were disappearing. Consequently in many colleges a relaxation of rules was under way or substantially completed. However, that was not the case at Oberlin. There a large body of rules minutely regulated all aspects of social relations. Because it was coeducational, Oberlin faced a problem unknown in most colleges. Coeducation was still an experiment, or at least many educators so professed to believe. Critics charged that coeducation at best led to distraction from studies and a concern with worldly distinctions while at worst it placed irresistible temptations before the young. The charges damaged a cause for which Oberlin stood and hurt its material prospects as well. Oberlin officials were determined that no sexual scandal should discredit either the cause or the College. Through a combination of strict social regulation and a positive religious environment, they hoped to avert such a calamity.

The rules, according to a statement in the Catalogue, were "few and simple, appealing to the student's self-respect and personal responsibility." All students were required to abstain from the use of tobacco and intoxicating drinks. The fundamental rule governing relations between the sexes read: "No student is allowed to visit one of the other sex at a private room, except by special permission in case of severe sickness." Women were required to be in their rooms after eight o'clock in the evening during the spring and summer months and after half-past seven during the fall and winter months. Men were required to be in their rooms by ten o'clock.[91]

These "few and simple" rules, however, were in actuality only the beginning. The College published booklets which informed the students of supplementary rules, particularly a large number that regulated the lives of the women and their relations with the men. Dancing and games of chance were prohibited. Attendance at approved social occasions, such as public lectures, picnics, and class socials, was carefully regulated. The library was sexually segregated in its operations, open at certain times only to men, at others only to women.[92] Rules governed, as to number and length, the calls young men paid on the women at their places of residence.[93] One rule forbade a man and a woman to converse by way of an open window. Another, easily evaded, prohibited men and women from walking together unless they were on urgent business that took them in the same direction. One observer recalled: "Happily a kind Providence had so ordered that when you *did* you always *were*." [94] Slow-motion walking was another way of avoiding violation of the letter of the law. The extreme form of this, according to two students, was "that slowest of all movements called the 'Oberlin step.'" With practice some couples could consume three minutes in crossing a single flagstone.[95]

In addition to the published rules, there were unprinted rules and interpretations of rules, characterized, so it was said, by such a "multiplicity and indefiniteness" that no two students understood them similarly, while "no Professor pretends to fathom them."[96] As one professor of the time later remarked, "it was thought inadvisable to print" them.[97] These fell within the province of Mrs. Adelia A. F. Johnston, or "Madame J," whose formidable nature was indicated by her sobriquet. As principal of the Ladies' Department from 1870 to 1894, she was chiefly responsible for the good conduct of the women. At the general exercises she conducted, which women were required to attend, she declared and interpreted this body of unwritten legislation and dealt with other matters pertaining to conduct and good form.[98]

To enforce the rules the officers and faculty relied upon a self-reporting system, supplemented by whatever information they could gather about student behavior, backed by the threat of disciplinary action. Students submitted regular reports listing their violations of the rules with their excuses. One student report read:

> Absent from prayers in the evening, twice, had business which I wished very much to do just then. Absent from church once, was *very tired* and had Union Ex. coming next day so left church after first hymn. Absent from Mon[thly] Rhetoricals the last time because of stress of work. Otherwise perfect.
>
> [signed] A. E. THOMASON [99]

Final disposition of disciplinary matters rested with the faculty. Although suspensions and even expulsions for flagrant or repeated violations and for false reporting were not unknown, and student editors occasionally found it necessary to exhort their fellows to obedience, College officials claimed that the great majority of students agreed that rules were necessary and abided by them.[100] Sometimes the disciplinary steps taken by those responsible seemed excessively harsh to others.[101] Apparently most cases in which discipline was required involved the younger preparatory department students rather than the students of the College.[102]

The maintenance of a strict system of rules and discipline just when many colleges and universities were liberalizing campus social life invited criticism and even ridicule. Disciplinary cases sometimes attracted the attention of the public through accounts in metropolitan and student newspapers. For example, when four men and two women were expelled in 1878 for "moonlight wanderings," the College was sharply criticized by the outside press.[103] The editors of the *Oberlin Review* were frequently obliged to defend the system of social regulation against the attacks of editors of student newspapers at other colleges.[104] The reputation of the College for strictness caused some new students to enter with misgivings. Agnes Fairchild, a niece of the president, wrote to her cousin, James T. Fairchild:

> Yes, I entend [*sic*] to board at the Hall and I hope they do have some fun there for I'm afraid it will seem like putting on a *very*

straight jacket [*sic*] going from here [Agnes' home was in Man-
hattan, Kansas] to Oberlin. I'm sure I'll enjoy it and mean to work
hard, and not disgrace the family name, but I can not live without
some amusement of some kind. . . . Are they very strict with the
girls after all? I'm not used to being cooped up but suppose I must
get used to it, and settle down to hard study. That is necessary
I find.[105]

Doubtless many students entered Oberlin expecting to lay aside
ordinary pleasures and conform to a new order.[106]

To encourage and sustain piety, College officials did not rely solely
on heavy-handed discipline. Rigorous and frequent application of
conventional evangelistic methods was of even greater importance in
the Oberlin scheme. As Shipherd, Stewart, and Finney had proclaimed, Oberlin should mold workers for the Lord who would by
instruction and example bring the people of the West to salvation.
So Oberlin life was permeated with study of the Scriptures, worship
services, prayer meetings, and religious lectures. Bible study courses,
which met an hour each week, were required of all students. Nearly
the entire Scriptures were carefully read during the four years of
undergraduate study. All students read the historical books of the
Old Testament and the poetical and prophetical books of the entire
Bible. Students in the Classical Course spent a year reading selections
from the New Testament in Greek. The course in theology called
System of Doctrines and that in Evidences of Christianity rounded
out the course requirements.[107]

Attendance at a great number of worship services was also required.
As in most colleges daily chapel was held, although at Oberlin, unlike
most, the students and faculty gathered for chapel in the late afternoon instead of early morning. Students sometimes complained that
the service lasted beyond the allotted fifteen minutes. When this
happened, many became "proportionally undevotional."[108] The desira-
bility of substituting voluntary for required chapel was seldom publicly
discussed. In lieu of a college morning service, prayers were offered
in the dormitories and private rooming and boarding houses. Students
were not permitted to live or board with families that did not offer
morning prayers.[109] They also had to attend preaching services both
Sunday morning and evening. They could attend any of the Protestant
churches in Oberlin—either of the two Congregationalist churches,
or the Methodist, Baptist, or Episcopal churches.[110] However, it was

expected that they would attend Congregationalist services unless they were members of a different denomination. The student was assisted in securing the largest benefit from these services by keeping distractions to a minimum. For many years no classes were scheduled on Monday so that students need not spend Sunday in preparing lessons, while travel and recreation on the Sabbath were strictly forbidden. Seventeen students were once punished—some suspended and others only reprimanded—for dishonoring the Sabbath with a game of baseball.[111]

In addition to these requirements there were customs that by long observance had attained the dignity of law. President Finney had contributed the practice of opening each class session with either a prayer or a hymn.[112] Faculty members who were gifted at praying usually chose to begin their classes in that way. As one student put it, "All our work is done by prayer."[113] In other classes a student was appointed to select hymns and lead the class in singing. The *Oberlin Review* confessed that these customs struck outsiders as peculiar.[114] In 1881 the editors of the paper engaged in a controversy with the editors of a Cornell University student newspaper who had claimed that a favorite pastime of Oberlin students was to place bets on the length of their professor's classroom prayers.[115] Although sensitive to the humor others found in praying and singing before class, the Oberlin editors defended their college's way. They often criticized students who were inattentive during prayer or a hymn. Too many, they claimed, used the time to whisper to neighbors or make last minute preparations for recitation.[116] Equally deplorable was the tendency of song leaders to select inappropriate hymns. So many of their selections were open to double meanings that the proper spirit of reverence was demolished.[117] Although hymn singing at the beginning of a class was in slight disrepute by the seventies, it did not die out until around the turn of the century. Another custom was the Thursday lecture, also a contribution of Finney.[118] It had been instituted to give those who could not hear the Sunday sermons of the great evangelist an opportunity to do so at a different time. In the sixties and seventies the lectures were delivered either by clerical faculty members or eminent visitors. In effect, the Thursday lecture was a third required sermon for the week.

Of nearly equal importance in creating the desired religious environment were the prayer meetings at which attendance was voluntary. Without great exaggeration it can be said that the Oberlin student could spend most of his time outside of class attending religious services. Of these the prayer meetings were the most numerous. A visitor to Oberlin reportedly remarked: "Why, if anyone walking along the sidewalks of Oberlin catches his foot and stumbles, nine chances out of ten, he stumbles into a prayer meeting." [119] Each college class had a prayer meeting on Friday afternoon. There were separate prayer meetings for men and women on Sunday evening and a weekly Young People's Prayer Meeting open to all students—college, preparatory, theological, and conservatory. Some of the faculty members who led these meetings regarded conducting them as their most valuable service to Oberlin students. Professor William G. Frost, for one, considered the Young People's Prayer Meeting, which he led, of greater benefit than his Greek classes.[120] Students were urged to make a decision for Christ and, in some meetings, conversions frequently occurred. Those who had experienced conversion testified to their faith and vowed to live a Christian life. In other meetings more emphasis was placed on the application of Christian principles to the problems of life with topics for study, texts from the Bible, and discussions.

Attendance at the meetings depended upon the skill of the leader, the season of the year, and other obligations of the students. Some meetings were well attended, others were largely ignored. The class prayer meetings and the union prayer meeting, which were among the few gatherings that men and women could jointly attend, seem to have been the most popular. The segregated men's and women's Sunday evening meetings were less attractive. In 1885 the *Oberlin Review* stated that the average student attended one prayer meeting each week.[121]

Two new religious organizations of importance appeared in the eighties. In 1881 a branch of the Young Men's Christian Association was founded. College Y.M.C.A.'s had been established on many campuses long before this.[122] The delay at Oberlin was due to the fact that its activities merely duplicated organizations and practices already in existence. The Y.M.C.A. was finally established to facilitate co-operation between Oberlin Christian students and those of other colleges.[123] The Oberlin organization grew very rapidly, reaching a membership of nearly four hundred by February, 1882, when it was said to be the largest college Y.M.C.A. in the world.[124] As in many coeducational colleges, the Oberlin Y.M.C.A. originally included women as well as men, but in 1894 a college Y.W.C.A. was established.[125] The Y.M.C.A. sponsored conversion campaigns like those of the prayer meetings. In November, 1883, meetings were held each night during a "week of prayer for young men."

> The meetings were opened with brief remarks by the leader, followed by singing, prayer and exhortations or experiences in quick succession, several persons frequently rising at the same moment. The services were brought to a close before the expiration of the hour and followed by an inquiry meeting. . . . While a number of teachers and members of the Y.M.C.A. were especially active, it is safe to say that a very large number of students received a fresh inspiration from the meetings, and about a hundred . . . have begun a Christian life. A few were systematically absent from all the services.[126]

Until the end of the century the Y.M.C.A. was simply another agency of conventional evangelicalism, with the difference that it was controlled by students.

The second new religious organization was the "class for the training of Christian workers" led by Henry C. King, associate professor of mathematics. Professor King began this work in 1884 at the request of a few young men.[127] A general topic for a year's study was proposed with readings in the Bible and commentaries, then in discussions the texts were applied to everyday situations. Evidently this class met a need since it soon became one of the most popular religious meetings with an average attendance of more than three hundred students. According to an editorial in the *Oberlin Review,* many who became active Christian workers after graduation found "the instruction and training they received in this class . . . the most valuable preparation for actual work of any they received in Oberlin."[128]

Finally, there were special religious observances such as the annual Day of Prayer for Colleges, which came in late January or early February. Classes were dismissed, and morning, afternoon, and evening services were held at which faculty members spoke and prayed. Depending upon the students' response and the other obligations of the students and faculty, the services sometimes continued for as long as a week. Attendance of students at the services of the

Day of Prayer was not required, but many students, as well as faculty and townspeople, gathered to worship. Some of the most moving Oberlin services were held on this day.[129] The regular round of services and meetings culminated in the revivals that occurred every three or four years during Fairchild's presidency. Oberlin revivals, it was claimed, were conducted on a high plane without "impassioned appeal and exhortation."[130] In January, 1877, the student newspaper reported that "the religious interest in the town and College is unusually great and is constantly increasing." There were days of fasting and prayer. Services were conducted each evening in the churches of Oberlin. Conversions were reported in the student prayer meetings, and a large, special prayer meeting was held in the chapel. "Among the students," the *Oberlin Review* reported, "there is a good deal of interest."[131] One resident of the town wrote that she had been to meeting almost every evening for three weeks and "had listened to the most *awfully* searching preaching."[132] At her church there were about one hundred conversions, and the newspaper later reported that there had been over two hundred in all.[133]

Another revival, sparked by the services on the Day of Prayer for Colleges, occurred in January and February of 1879. All of the class prayer meetings were the scene of conversions. The Reverend Josiah Strong was brought to the campus to preach. One professor wrote: "We are right in the midel [*sic*]—I hope only the beginning—of a grand revival; already a great many of the most difficult cases among the students, have been reached and brought to Christ. We hope the work will spread and bring in the townfolks also."[134] A student reported that the "big revival" lasted almost two months and resulted in over sixty conversions, "some very striking cases too."[135] In his annual report, Fairchild declared that "a healthful religious interest has been manifest during the year—more conspicuously during the last winter, when a large number, from all classes, entered upon the Christian life."[136] The president customarily commented on the religious state of the students in his annual reports but not always did he have such gratifying news to impart.

The revivals and other religious services helped to create an evangelical community. Oberlin probably contained as large a proportion of practicing Christian students as any college in the country.

In 1881 President Fairchild claimed that seven of every eight students in the Classical Course either were members of Protestant denominations or had indicated a serious personal interest in religion which, it was expected, would soon lead to active membership.[137] The large number of Oberlin graduates who devoted themselves to Christian service of various kinds testified to the sincerity of their belief and the effectiveness of the means for inculcating dedication relied upon by officials. More Oberlin male graduates between 1877 and 1886— 25 per cent of the total—chose religious work, as minister or missionary, than any other vocation.[138] As one student wrote home in a letter, "You never saw such a religeous [sic] place."[139]

The evangelical mission of early Oberlin required more than indoctrination of students in Christian beliefs. The test of faith lay in good works. The founders hoped that Oberlin's graduates would carry the message of salvation to people everywhere. The conventional expression of this obligation was missionary activity. Throughout the nineteenth century Oberlin students were engaged on many fronts in the battle with religious heresy, ignorance, and indifference. Oberlin missionaries went to Canada and Jamaica to work with refugee slaves and freedmen. The Mendi mission was founded on the western coast of Africa to carry the gospel to the Negroes. The Indian tribes of northern Minnesota were an object of attention before the Civil War.[140] To supervise and support the activities of these various missions Oberlin graduates helped to found, in 1846, the American Missionary Association. This association—strongly antislavery before the Civil War and deeply involved in work for the freedman during Reconstruction—was in large part an Oberlin enterprise.[141] In 1881 an Oberlin group founded a mission in Shansi province in China with the support of the American Board of Commissioners of Foreign Missions. Henceforth most Oberlin missionary interest was directed overseas. One estimate holds that by the close of the century Oberlin had sent about one thousand missionaries to both foreign and domestic fields.[142]

Even this missionary movement did not exhaust the evangelical impulse. The founders thought that students and townspeople should be exemplars of piety as well as promoters of missionary enterprises. In their judgment, the people of the American west and of the world needed the model of Christian dedication and behavior that Oberlin could provide.

The arrangements of Oberlin community and college life were designed to aid weak mankind in resisting sinful temptations. Of all the current threats to virtue, none seemed greater than drink, a position made plausible by the immense amount of spirits consumed in the old West. The early Covenant of the colony, signed by the original settlers, banned the use of "all strong and unnecessary drinks." Some early Oberlin residents argued that tea and coffee were covered by this prohibition; all agreed that it included intoxicants. The College, for its part, required a pledge from all men to use neither intoxicants nor tobacco.[143] Although violations of the tobacco rule seem to have occurred with some regularity, neither the tobacco nor the drink ban was seriously challenged until the twentieth century. Throughout the nineteenth century these rules were supported or acquiesced in by the great majority of students.

Maintaining the purity of the community was a more formidable challenge.[144] The community at large was much less homogeneous than the select group of college students, and the townspeople could not be subjected in the same manner and degree to paternalistic authority. Yet college officials and their sympathizers among the townspeople considered a dry community essential to Oberlin's success as an evangelical institution. The calm of village life was broken by a series of "temperance wars" in the seventies and early eighties through which they sought, by a variety of methods, to prevent the sale of liquor in Oberlin. These campaigns came to a head in 1881–82 when four men tried to open the town to the liquor traffic. One establishment was nominally a drug store, one a hotel, and two were groceries; but, so the *Oberlin Review* claimed, all were "grog-shops." [145] Oberlin quickly rallied against the threat: "Committees were appointed to speak to the saloon keepers and endeavor to persuade them to give up the traffic and volunteers were called for to go to the men and talk and labor with them. Meanwhile prayer-meetings were held every afternoon in the Reading Room and mass meetings twice a week in the churches." [146] Fights broke out at "the obnoxious drug store" between local toughs and students.[147] All of the offenders eventually pledged themselves not to sell liquor, but this proved to be only a respite.[148] In the winter and spring of 1882 the prohibitionist ranks were reformed: "Committees have visited the drug store hourly and it is hoped will succeed before long in causing the sale of liquor to cease."[149] President Fairchild spoke the thoughts of many when he declared at a large meeting of townspeople and students:

> We are fighting the demon of the land in his only stronghold among us. . . . The drug store which is the center of so much interest here and the object of more or less sympathy abroad is the place where the liquor business . . . has been carried on for many years. . . . We are not fanatics but we are in earnest.[150]

The crusaders were sometimes insulted. When a group of prohibitionists called at the drug store, two young men deliberately puffed tobacco smoke in their faces. The two culprits were arrested, tried, and fined for assault by the local authorities.[151] The struggle ended when the drug store, along with several other buildings, burned down on March 6, 1882. According to the *Oberlin Review*, the fire started in a nearby butcher's shop, but, it added, there was "much speculation" on its origin.[152]

The victory was secured when the Ohio General Assembly passed prohibition legislation in March, 1882. Named for George P. Metcalf, the representative of Oberlin's legislative district, the new law authorized the councils of college and university towns to pass effective prohibition ordinances. The Oberlin Temperance Alliance, which had long favored such legislation, sent Professor James Monroe, a powerful advocate, to Columbus to lobby for the measure.[153] As a former state representative, United States Congressman, and diplomat, Monroe was wise in the ways of legislative bodies and a respected figure among Ohio Republicans. When the news of the bill's passage was announced at chapel, the "applause of the students, the ringing of the old bell, and the wave of enthusiasm that spread through the town evinced the joy with which it was received."[154] A town ordinance was soon passed that successfully prohibited all liquor retailing.

The identity of interest between the town and the College was most evident in the anti-liquor crusade. The local temperance organization officers included, at various times, President Fairchild, Giles W. Shurtleff, Judson Smith, John M. Ellis, and Frank F. Jewett from the College, while many students zealously supported the movement.

The ministers of Oberlin's churches and some businessmen were also prominent. Both the community and the College wanted to maintain a reputation for purity. In College publications this was held up as a reassurance to parents of prospective students. As the catalogue stated, Oberlin was

> a pleasant and healthful village. . . . The place was founded as a home for the College, and the population consists chiefly of those who have been drawn there by educational attractions. This gives it a special atmosphere of culture and good order, while as a home for students it is remarkably free from the temptations and dangers often surrounding school life. There are no drinking saloons in town.[155]

James H. Fairchild was president of Oberlin from 1866 until 1889. Through approximately the first fifteen years of his term of service the College was still that of the founders, united around its evangelical tradition and commitment.[156] This faith was exact and explicit; as an evangelical college Oberlin knew its mind and had few doubts of the lasting validity of its religious principles. They fostered an earnest and sober dedication among students. Students' words, deeds, and thoughts were never far from the Lord's work in this world and their eternal abode in the next. The application of the evangelical principle largely precluded social pretension and exclusiveness since, consistently and rigorously applied, it judged all impartially by the worthiness of their belief and character. Manifestations of this were to be found in the opposition to the establishment of fraternities, the absence of overt snobbery, the aid to poor students, and the absence of racial discrimination.[157] All worked together to create the kind and degree of dedication desired. Learning, held deliberately in subjection to the claims of religion, was the weakest element of the evangelical college. Formal studies were rigid in prescription, limited in scope, antiquated in method, and sometimes superficial in content. Despite the fact that President Fairchild apparently saw little need for reform, Oberlin in the eighties began slowly and cautiously to move toward new outlooks on its educational, social, and religious objectives.

## CHAPTER II

# THE EVANGELICAL COLLEGE IN TRANSITION

President Fairchild hoped Oberlin would always conform to the hallowed academic, religious, and social patterns delineated in his inaugural address. New currents were running in American life, however, and the exertions of many men, at Oberlin as elsewhere, were insufficient to maintain an absolute adherence to the traditions of the old college. Most new academic modes found a comfortable setting in the universities where the untrammeled pursuit of scientific and humanistic knowledge, the cultivation of objective judgment, and experiments with the curriculum all flourished.[1] New or renovated institutions seized academic leadership. Setting the pace of academic innovation were Charles W. Eliot at Harvard University, Andrew D. White at Cornell, Daniel Coit Gilman at Johns Hopkins, and, later in the century, William Rainey Harper and David Starr Jordan at Chicago and Stanford. As the universities tried new ways of serving American society, the old colleges were forced to take stock.

The colleges responded to this challenge of new needs, ideas, and institutions as best they could. A few advanced eagerly toward university status; some turned inward; others marked time while awaiting a reform administration or larger financial resources; most fashioned a compromise between old and new. The latter course, while seldom entirely satisfactory, did enable colleges to survive in a competitive situation and to maintain their integrity by upholding historic principles as steadfastly as prudence dictated and necessity allowed. By the time of Fairchild's resignation from the presidency in 1889, Oberlin had begun to fashion its response to new religious, social, and academic expectations. There had been no violent wrench with the past, but in many ways Oberlin was no longer the college of the founders. The desire to glorify God and mold man in His image still consecrated the labors of teachers and students. The individualistic evangelicalism of Shipherd and Finney, however, no longer dominated Oberlin's consciousness.

No part of institutional life was fully insulated from the forces of change. Even the composition and structure of the board of trustees reflected dependence upon a more diversified culture and constituency. By 1878 the number of trustees had been increased to twenty-four, and since the alumni had been authorized to select six members, the board was no longer entirely self-perpetuating.[2] This new procedure, giving the alumni greater direct influence in college affairs, brought to the board a significant number of spokesmen for academic reform.

In most important respects, the trustees of 1889—Fairchild's last year in office—were more diverse than those of 1866. A slight majority, fourteen of the twenty-four, were residents of Ohio, but this was a far smaller proportion of Ohioans than the board had contained in 1866. The distribution of occupations among trustees had also significantly changed. The number of clergymen, five of twelve trustees in 1866, had shrunk to four out of twenty-four by 1889, with business and professional men increasing in proportion. If Oberlin's president was still a minister, he now had few professional colleagues on the board. Among the lay members of the board, however, there still were many who were noted as much for philanthropies as for business or professional accomplishments.[3] The disappearance of certain customs of the board perhaps reflects the decline in the number and influence of clergymen. In the early years of Fairchild's presidency the trustees collectively were often referred to as "Brethren" in the minutes, and board meetings were always opened with prayer. After 1875 the title was not used, while board meetings began with prayer only on critical occasions when a president was chosen or severe financial problems faced.[4] More and more, the decisions about Oberlin's future rested with alumni. Only three of the trustees of 1866 had been college graduates, but by 1889, twelve, of whom ten were Oberlin graduates, had earned degrees.[5]

The College faculty of 1889, more than the board, reflected new academic and cultural expectations.[6] Only two of the faculty members of 1866—John M. Ellis and Charles H. Churchill—were still in service, although James Monroe, who had been on the faculty before 1866, had resumed teaching in 1883 after a long interlude in politics and diplomacy. Monroe, Ellis, and Churchill formed an ante bellum remnant. Many of the new faculty members, it is true, carried on old traditions. Five of the fourteen faculty members had received all of their training at Oberlin, being graduates of both College and seminary. Five more had received a part of their training—either collegiate or theological—at Oberlin. Only four teachers had been educated entirely in other institutions, and three of these had joined the faculty as recently as 1888 and 1889. Charles Harris, Professor of German, who had studied at the University of Leipzig, was the only Oberlin professor who had earned the degree of Doctor of Philosophy. Among the others, advanced preparation consisted of work in theological schools and a few earned Master of Arts degrees.[7]

The ten out of fourteen faculty members in 1889 who were either partially or wholly trained at Oberlin, when contrasted with the eight of nine in 1866, reflected a faculty with a more varied training and experience. Although recent appointments revealed a willingness to seek and hire men trained elsewhere, many faculty and alumni still advocated the policy of hiring Oberlin graduates. The defenders of the past recognized that the preservation of the evangelical character of Oberlin was bound up with a faculty pledged to the historic religious commitment, and they feared the dangers of a secular knowledge entirely outside the framework of religious faith and purpose. One young clerical alumnus urged the strengthening of the "evangelical idea of the College" through careful faculty appointments, declaring: "More and more I feel the utter uselessness of un-religious culture."[8] Professor William G. Frost, a vigorous faculty champion of Oberlin evangelicalism, wrote: "We *must* have Oberlin candidates for Oberlin places."[9] He feared that teachers trained elsewhere came to Oberlin not to learn from its tradition and accept its principles but to undermine them by contempt and closed minds. In praising the "evangelistic, reformatory, missionary type of religion for which Oberlin exists," Frost yielded to none.[10] Those alumni and faculty who agreed with Frost often wrote to President Fairchild and other representatives of evangelical conservatism urging them to keep Oberlin true to the old ways.[11]

Some students and teachers, on the other hand, urged the broadening of Oberlin's faculty through the appointment of graduates of other institutions. As early as 1874 a student writing in the *Oberlin Review* questioned the reasoning used in support of faculty inbreeding and indirectly attacked the conception of education as religious in-doctrination. The argument was stated in general terms, but doubtless readers were expected to make a particular application. The author claimed that challenges to the "fixed set of ideas in matters of discipline, of morals, of manners, and upon all the questions arising in a college course" would come about only as new instructors were brought into a college.[12] Admittedly this was difficult in "poverty-stricken colleges, where the faculty are paid starvation salaries, and each member is required to do the work of three or four men," but no progress could be made unless new men were added to the faculty. The tendency toward intellectual confinement was aggravated by those parents who insisted that their children attend their own college. With instructors and students reared in similar settings, "the method changes from an investigation, common to all, to dogmatic assertion on the one hand, and passive receptivity on the other." Some enterprising and fortunate students sought a more varied intellectual fare by changing colleges midway through their course; those who remained should insist that "new men—men educated else-where—shall be appointed to fill vacancies."[13]

Another indication of a new conception of the teacher's responsi-bilities was the enhanced status of advanced training. Oberlin gradu-ates marked for college positions acquired graduate training elsewhere before beginning their teaching.[14] Nearly all of the young men who joined the faculty in the eighties had at least several months or years of advanced work, although not all had earned advanced degrees. Even some experienced teachers were encouraged to secure advanced training. In 1888, Lyman B. Hall, who had been teaching Latin since 1872, was granted a leave of absence with salary for a year's study in Germany.[15] The need for specialized training was now recognized by many faculty members, officials, and trustees. The old notion that any man of correct religion, worthy character, native intelligence, and a command of the rudiments of a subject could be a successful teacher was slowly dying.

One of the younger members of the faculty was Harry Huntington Powers, professor of French, whose career at Oberlin from 1888 to 1892 illustrates some of the threats to evangelical unity posed by new instructors. Since he had been educated at the University of Wisconsin and at the Sorbonne, the *Oberlin Review* thought him "eminently fitted for the position."[16] Although he was an able and immensely popular teacher, his relations with his colleagues were somewhat strained because of his ideas and his manner of expressing them. Shortly after Powers arrived, one colleague observed: "The new French professor seems aggressive and too outspoken for a politic man. I think the President will 'see' him either in faculty meeting or outside." [17] Powers stirred debate on a number of issues that would scarcely have been raised earlier. His religion was unorthodox. His humanitarian conception of Jesus provoked a "lively debate" within the faculty, and he spread his views in a "large and earnest" student Bible class.[18] In a lecture to students and faculty on "Prophets and Pharisees," he rebuked narrow orthodoxy and religious affectation. One member of the faculty judged the lecture "conceited and defiant in tone and reckless of its influence upon students." [19] This influence was so feared that a spokesman for orthodoxy, Professor George F. Wright of the theological seminary, delivered a rejoinder which, according to one observer, was "earnest but light in substance." [20]

On many other issues Powers took advanced positions. He aligned himself with those who believed Oberlin should cast loose from its evangelical moorings in order to develop as a university.[21] His views on social and political questions were as unorthodox as his religious beliefs. In 1893 he contributed to the *Oberlin Review* a utopian fantasy entitled "A Pedagogue in Wonderland," probably inspired by Edward Bellamy's recently published *Looking Backward*.[22] In it an Oberlin professor, asleep for one hundred years, awoke to find the College and town remarkably changed. All of the institutions and principles of social life were judged by their contributions to the public welfare. In conversations with the inhabitants, the teacher discovered that the pure capitalism of his day had been found unworkable and dangerous. Industrial trusts and the "right to own" had enslaved the people. Armed rebellion had finally ended suffering and social injustice, whereupon co-operation, or "the application of Christianity to the social and material life of society," was substituted for individualism as an organizing principle. Private property and capitalism, although not abolished, had been brought under strict public control.[23]

Professor Powers was anything but a typical faculty member of the late eighties; rather he illustrates the greater variety in views and temperament that had entered the old college. In 1892 he left Oberlin to return to the University of Wisconsin to study political economy with Professor Richard T. Ely. As an open dissenter from Oberlin orthodoxy he had represented a minority.

A sharper and more sustained criticism of the old college came from a few of the students. They pointed out deficiencies in Oberlin's educational practices and sometimes suggested improvements which the faculty chose not to ignore. A recurring charge indicted the superficial quality of instruction. In too many courses only the rudiments of a subject were surveyed. One editorial in the *Oberlin Review* asserted that many of the better students left Oberlin before graduation to complete their studies elsewhere because of this defect. The writer thought the loss of good students could be prevented by the addition of many elective courses and of new, better trained teachers.[24] In a similar editorial it was suggested that admission standards be raised so that instruction in secondary subjects would not have to be provided. Raising admission standards, the writer claimed, "would give our institution a much better position among the colleges of the country," without significantly lowering the number of entrants.[25]

No student critic directly attacked the evangelical commitment of the College as an obstacle to academic improvement, but some did declare that intellectual standards had been dangerously neglected in favor of maintaining the desired moral and religious environment. The pursuit of spiritual ends, so it was said, was not a valid excuse for low academic standards. As a student writer declared:

> Oberlin has won its name and its countless multitude of warm friends, by seeking the practical development of the man, by giving that which is really of paramount value the highest place. The danger, of course, is to undervalue mere intellectual attainments, to consider that which is really of subordinate value, but still of high value, as being of too little worth. There is need that, while we cling to the rich spiritual life which we have, we reach out and strive for high intellectual attainments.[26]

In particular this writer criticized the College for failing to appoint men to its faculty who had secured advanced training. All first-class colleges, he stated, had some teachers who had been trained in foreign universities, a standard that pointedly excluded Oberlin from the highest rank.[27]

In a more biting editorial, another student accused the "sectarian" colleges of trying to educate by dogmatic methods, an impossibility since doubt was the only true educator. The College needed new men with new ideas "for it seems inevitable that one who has taught for many years in the same channel should become intolerant of contradiction, while natural indolence on the part of many pupils leads them to accept without question the dictum of whomsoever their teachers may be." [28] So dogmatism dominated education, while doubt, the stimulus to investigation and the necessary condition of scholarship, was suppressed. Students, careless or indifferent, were as guilty as professors. "How often do answers seem to be framed to fit the well known view of the Professor!" [29] The spirit of doubt, among both students and teachers, was said to be indispensable to academic progress at Oberlin. In a similar article on "The College of the Future," another student attacked the restrictions on thought and conviction implicit in fidelity to a single set of ideas. Rigid loyalty to a system curtailed original investigation, the only way in which students could arrive at truth.[30] By the close of Fairchild's presidency in 1889, the unsettling propositions that doubt must precede knowledge and that only detached and patient investigation could lead to truth had defenders among Oberlin students, foreshadowing a new relationship between religion and learning.

In defense of innovation, some students appealed to the pioneering past of Oberlin. In one of many discussions of the controversial question of elective courses, the editors of the *Oberlin Review* argued that conservatism in educational matters was overtaking a college that had been known as a radical institution.[31] Oberlin's earlier radicalisms, such as abolitionism and coeducation, had been vindicated. Danger lurked in "our being satisfied with the achievements of the past, and of lapsing into a state of conservatism." [32] Maintaining that the challenges of the day were academic in nature, the writer argued that Oberlin, if true to its character, must permit students some choice of subjects. Another student writer criticized the College for "a great readiness to lie back on its laurels and let the educational interests take care of themselves." [33] The easy way was to replace departed professors with men of only equal or even lesser ability. The aim, however, should be to appoint men of greater ability and reputation: "When new professors are elected they should be men of vast learning and world-wide fame. . . . Oberlin's students demand that the College shall be placed on a level with the best colleges of the land, and it is not impossible." [34] Although it would be necessary to pay much larger salaries than were current at Oberlin, the writer believed this could be done. Another student deplored the fact that so few Oberlin professors published scholarly articles and books. The needs of the future could be met only by a more profound scholarship, he said, to which Oberlin teachers were making little or no contribution. "Oberlin's rougher battles are fought. Why in these more peaceful days should she not let her philosophical and literary excellence be known? We think that the influence of our college might be extended and its reputation advanced in the way we have indicated." [35] The students apparently saw no reason to exempt Oberlin itself from the injunction to judge institutions and experiences.

Developments in other academic institutions proved to be a useful source of ideas and standards. Students and faculty members frequently contrasted Oberlin with eastern colleges and universities in articles in the student newspaper. Differences in standards of admission, the elective system, student piety, school spirit, student deportment, expenses, faculty salaries, and even the size and variety of stuffed animal collections were all elaborately described and analyzed.[36] Recent students and graduates, visiting or attending eastern colleges, frequently submitted letters and articles contrasting the academic work and student life of those institutions with Oberlin. These commentaries often struck a judicious balance by praising the high moral standards of Oberlin and the scholarship of other institutions.[37] German universities as well as some of their new American counterparts furnished a particularly rigorous standard by which to measure the American college. Among Oberlin students of the eighties there was great interest in university aims, methods, and developments at home and abroad. In 1880 the *Oberlin Review*, listing the activities of the members of the Class of 1879, noted that "Heazleton writes enthusiastically from Göttingen." [38] In an article on "Zoological Studies in the German Universities," emphasizing the encouragement given to original scientific investigations there, a student writer urged the addition of laboratory science courses at Oberlin.[39] The German universities were praised as the acme of academic accomplishment. Their freedom of investigation and study accounted for much of Germany's progress and placed them among the marvels of the modern world. American universities, one editorial concluded, could do no better than carefully emulate them.[40]

Also in the eighties a significant number of Oberlin graduates began to enter American universities for advanced work. Their progress was often closely followed by student and faculty friends at Oberlin. Johns Hopkins University was a favorite for these Oberlin students.[41] The Oberlin contingent of seven students in 1888 was the largest delegation to that university from any one college.[42] Oberlin alumni at Johns Hopkins praised its work. As one wrote to an Oberlin professor: "I am greatly pleased with my studies and with this institution. Every opportunity, I believe, is here afforded for students to improve their minds, to store knowledge of every sort, to carry on the investigation of any scientific truth, and to fit themselves for their future usefulness."[43] The university was highly regarded for cultivating careful, deep inquiry, and for uniting scholarship with the study of important public questions.[44] The German and American universities were beginning to have a significant impact on the academic goals of Oberlin and on the careers of its graduates. They were both an institutional and a personal liberating force. By means of university study and experience, Oberlin graduates promoted a higher academic stature for their alma mater.

The earnestness and serious purpose of Oberlin students, once directed almost exclusively to the attainment of evangelical aims, were increasingly being brought to bear on intellectual training and discipline. Perhaps this reflected a new awareness of the intricacy of modern life. As Americans began to emerge from a time of innocence and isolation, the simple affirmations of the past became nebulous and lost their relevance. The satisfaction of individual and social needs in the future would require a more exacting attention to careful and persistent intellectual inquiry and analysis. To be of service, students must, with inquisitive minds, attain a greater mastery of knowledge. The educational plan of Oberlin had not been designed primarily to facilitate such an accomplishment, but, thanks in large part to student awareness of new needs, the College was forced to undertake academic reform.

The last half of President Fairchild's presidency, or from 1875 to 1889, was a period of unusual academic progress. The pace of change seemed slow to advocates of a more rapid advance, but the first steps toward the creation of a college of high academic standing were taken. No one proposed the abandonment of evangelicalism. Still "mere intellectual attainment," so often placed in opposition to evangelicalism, now seemed to be a worthy and necessary if still subordinate goal. A first need was to undermine the sanctity of the prescribed curriculum, thereby opening the course of study to new subjects that could be taught with detachment and objectivity. Until the incrusted curriculum was broken, courses incorporating new knowledge and new approaches to knowledge could not be taught. When President Charles W. Eliot in his inaugural address in 1869 announced his intention to introduce an elective system at Harvard, he made this old question the pre-eminent issue among American educators.[45] At Oberlin the fixed curriculum of the liberal arts college had never been regarded as sacrosanct. The founders had freely modified the course of study in their desire to serve God, although no significant departure from the standard curriculum had actually taken place.[46] The obstacles to course changes and greater flexibility were perhaps not so strong as they were at some colleges. Oberlin student writings on the curriculum were unanimous in urging an experiment with election. The theory of "mental discipline," used by the defenders of prescribed courses, was branded a "hackneyed phrase" irrelevant to proper academic aims. Education should "prepare [the student's] mind for the course of life," which could be done only through a degree of specialization in studies. The introduction of elective courses, it was argued, would invigorate teaching since instructors would have to attract students by their ability.[47]

In July, 1875, the faculty and board of trustees decided to introduce a "scheme of elective studies."[48] The "scheme" initially was quite limited, consisting only of permitting the juniors to choose between a course in Greek, in which Plato's *Phaedo* was read, and a German course in which they would read Goethe's *Hermann und Dorothea*. The *Oberlin Review* commended the innovation, hopefully saying: "We are glad to see this indication of a disposition on the part of the Faculty to open the door as fast as possible for the introduction of the 'New Education.'"[49] Actually, the faculty moved slowly in introducing a selection of studies. Throughout Fairchild's presidency all of the subjects of the freshman year, which included Greek, Latin, mathematics (mainly trigonometry and analytical geometry), and introductory physics, were required.[50] Until 1885 most of the upperclass courses were prescribed, but the student could add to the requirements from a short list of electives. In that year a large number of new elective courses for upperclassmen were added. Courses in chemistry, botany, astronomy, psychology, Rhetoric, logic, Christian evidences, ethics, and modern history were still required, but the rest of the student's courses were elective. Although the faculty agreed to enlarge the list of electives in 1885, and the courses henceforth were listed in the catalogue, implementation required the addition of several instructors which the College was not immediately able to supply.[51] Eventually the new plan made it possible for upperclassmen to choose from a great variety of courses in many different fields.[52]

Many disciplines expanded in the new era of permissiveness. As a strong student demand for courses in the modern languages, the natural sciences, and the social sciences prompted a dramatic expansion of those fields, the old curriculum of ancient languages and philosophical-religious studies slowly gave way. The value of modern language study had long been recognized, but the College, before the seventies, had made only irregular gestures toward providing instruction.[53] James K. Newton, appointed instructor in French and German in 1873 and promoted to professor in 1875, taught at Oberlin until 1888.[54] Although Newton was a poor speaker and an unpopular teacher, he was an aggressive advocate of modern language study.[55] In a Thursday lecture before the student body he argued that modern literature contained accounts and interpretations of human experience which easily bore comparison with the classics of the ancient languages. He proposed that the opportunities for the study of modern languages be increased as rapidly as possible.[56] In another Thursday lecture he suggested that the study of the ancient languages be postponed until the modern languages had been mastered. To the Oberlin Latin professor, this was "a foolish idea very weakly presented but to my amazement the students seem much impressed by it."[57] By 1887 the growing demand for courses in German justified the appointment of an additional teacher, Charles Harris, and he soon had to be assisted by another teacher, Charles B. Martin, who had originally been appointed to teach the ancient languages.[58] The competition of modern languages stimulated instruction in the ancient languages.

One Oberlin student had gone so far as to lay the blame for the monotony of student social life on the close, grammatical study of the ancient classics, subjects "of so little vitality" that they "naturally tend to dry up and shrivel our social nature." [59] Although the teachers of the ancient languages sometimes despaired of their subjects' prospects in competition with the modern foreign languages, they tried to make their courses more attractive and beneficial by laying greater stress upon literary and humanistic values. [60] By 1888 President Fairchild, somewhat optimistically, claimed that the ancient languages "bid fair to hold their own," with the new aims and methods of instruction that had been adopted. [61]

The rapid expansion in foreign languages was followed at a distance by new studies in the related subjects of English language, literature, and rhetoric. If students were to be knowledgeable in the literature of foreign cultures, it was argued, they should be equally familiar with classic writings in their own tongue. [62] The College had long provided some instruction in rhetoric, although it was claimed by students that membership in a literary society provided better preparation for public speaking. Each student presented an oration at Monthly Rhetoricals once every year. These exercises were supervised, often inadequately, by an instructor whose primary duties were in another discipline. [63] In 1881 the College fulfilled the hopes of several generations of students by appointing an instructor in elocution who gave weekly lessons and exercises. [64] In English literature instruction was even more meager. Professor John M. Ellis, among his many other duties, delivered a short series of lectures to seniors with recitations from John Bascom's text on the subject. This was regarded by students as wholly inadequate. [65] In 1881 President Fairchild and the faculty recommended that a professor of English literature be appointed whenever financial resources permitted, which did not occur until 1889 when Professor William I. Thomas was added to the faculty. Only then was English literature properly established as a collegiate study. [66]

Although the proper distribution of study in the languages provoked student interest and some controversy within the faculty, instruction in philosophy and the sciences and the relation of knowledge in those subjects to religious faith were potentially far more divisive issues.

Already some of the traditional features of evangelical Christianity were being subjected to criticism. The process of replacing the old content of evangelicalism with new doctrines and practices was under way. Some students, then as perhaps always, obeyed the rules in spite of their own wishes. As one undergraduate wrote to his parents: "I go to church on the Sabbath (because I have to) and put Father's money in the contribution box." [67] Compulsory attendance at daily chapel was questioned, to be sure only rarely, on the grounds that coercion in worship was inappropriate and ineffective. [68] One student remembered the requirements as a "straitcoat" which constricted intellectual and religious interests. [69] Occasionally some students charged that the strong pressures toward religious affirmation had destructive consequences. Religious zeal, they said, sometimes led the faithful to self-defeating extremes in their dealings with others. The round of services and prayer metings, in addition to class work, could produce a mental and physical strain that only a very remarkable constitution could bear. If some students chose not to participate fully they should not be subjected to excessive inquiry. Students were warned to guard against "an immoderate zeal and intemperate enthusiasm," which could lead to unwarranted interference in the lives of others. [70]

The effectiveness of Oberlin religious methods and the reliability of statistical measurements of piety were called into question. According to one student writer, a close observer of Oberlin students could detect a surprising degree of skepticism of the doctrines of orthodox Christianity. A superficial glance at the number of religious services, the statistics of church membership, and attendance at religious exercises was misleading. [71] The pressure to accept orthodoxy, the writer continued, caused students to hide their skepticism from all but closest friends. Mischief resulted when teachers and officers failed to bring doubt into the open in order to help the student resolve it. Since the official attitude was that skepticism simply did not exist, the troubled student had few opportunities for free discussion of religious and philosophical questions. Almost without exception the religious services were "places in which the doubter is, to put it mildly, thanked for keeping silent; in which to boldly avow one's disbelief is regarded as equivalent to an attempt to scatter heresy. Religious doubts among thinking people cannot be prevented. The only question is, how can they be removed?"[72] The writer believed that both voluntary and compulsory religious services were utterly inadequate for that purpose.

The philosophy courses, particularly the course in Moral Philosophy usually taught by President Fairchild, might have served as a forum for the discussion of controversial religious questions. They were not, however, used for that purpose. According to his biographer, Fairchild sought to cover in the course the "whole range of individual and national life and . . . to make everything Christian and sane," in order "to develop manhood and to secure Christian service in their wider relationships."[73] He attempted to state the fundamental and eternal "laws of Being," those universal religious principles relating man to God which Fairchild subsumed under the "law of benevolence."[74] Some students saw the object of the philosophy courses as the inculcation of evangelical orthodoxy. As one editorial in the *Oberlin Review* stated: "It seems to be thought that the sole object of psychological, ethical and kindred studies is to indoctrinate the pupil, and therefore the instruction in these branches is put into the hands of a 'safe' member of the faculty, who is expected to lead his flock into 'safe' metaphysical pastures."[75] This student held that the teaching of philosophy should nurture a philosophical spirit—the quest for truth and wisdom. Students, he claimed, were naturally drawn to such an enterprise, but a rigid "didactic posture" by the instructor discouraged independent thinking.[76] Similar editorials occasionally appeared in the *Oberlin Review* throughout the later years of Fairchild's presidency, a number sufficient to indicate that at least some thoughtful students believed that the teaching of philosophy at Oberlin was sorrowfully defective.[77] One faculty member privately expressed the opinion "that the work in philosophy in Oberlin is the most hopelessly behind the times."[78]

Two brilliant students of the eighties, close friends and classmates Henry Northrup Castle and George Herbert Mead, were critics of Oberlin philosophy teaching. Mead later taught philosophy for many years at the University of Chicago; Castle, described by an Oberlin teacher as one of the two most brilliant intellects he had encountered, pursued philosophical studies at Harvard and several German universities before his early death.[79] Castle and Mead delighted in putting difficult philosophical questions to President Fairchild which "that dear old gentleman" usually failed to answer.[80] Although they had a high regard for Fairchild's character, neither had a similar regard for his ability as a teacher of philosophy.[81] Mead later wrote of the instruction they received: "We had nothing really constructive, for the aim of the philosophy taught was to do away with the need of any and all speculation." In the spring of 1882, with the confidence of juniors, they decided that a dogmatic philosophy was beyond the grasp of man. In the following year, "the classes in philosophy became a series of running fights with the professor. It was a new and magnificent game, a sort of border warfare, in which we feared no serious invasions of our own territory. The enemy was bound to a defensive system, and we congratulated ourselves on many a successful incursion." [82] Oberlin's other philosopher, Professor John M. Ellis, received similar treatment. Mead and Castle found Professor Ellis in his courses Mental Philosophy and Evidences of Christianity somewhat more tolerant of disturbing inquiries but, in their judgment, scarcely any more capable of providing convincing answers.[83] These students were not persuaded by the official rationale of philosophy teaching—the theory of indoctrination. The weakness of the theory could lead to a questioning of the whole system of encouraging positive religious conviction.

Another religious and philosophical course, called Systems of Doctrine, was taught by Professor Judson Smith. It consisted of a study of Bishop Joseph Butler's *The Analogy of Religion Natural and Revealed to the Constitution and Course of Nature.* According to one student Professor Smith required that "the students get it word for word, almost." [84] This course was commonly regarded as a stumbling block because of the professor's dry, exacting methods and his unreceptiveness to criticism of the bishop's arguments.[85] "It was purely memory work, with no questions and no promptings." [86] Students also complained that the *Analogy,* first published in 1736, was outmoded. The work could not meet all of the objections to Christian doctrine that sprang from a thoroughgoing materialistic philosophical position. As one student put it: "We plead . . . that Butler's place be filled by a theologian suited to meet the wants of students in the nineteenth rather than the seventeenth century. The flint-lock and the cross-bow are poor weapons against Springfield rifles and Gatling guns." [87] In 1884, with Professor Smith's departure from Oberlin, the study of the *Analogy* was discontinued. [88]

Behind much of this student unhappiness with evangelically inspired courses and rules lay the challenge to orthodoxy contained in the evolutionary hypothesis. Although the general concept of evolutionary development had long been known to scientists, the publication of Charles Darwin's *Origin of Species* in 1859, providing support for the theory of natural selection with a mass of evidence, brought biological evolution as the best scientific hypothesis into the public consciousness for the first time. The impact was soon felt in religious and educational circles in the United States. Controversy raged over a variety of issues either raised directly or taken as implications of this new learning.

Articulate Oberlin students by and large responded more favorably than the faculty to the new theory. One issue and one implication of evolution received particular attention. The issue was the relation between Christian faith and evolutionary science: Did acceptance of evolution preclude evangelical beliefs? Was Darwinism tantamount to infidelity? In the 1870's, as the scientific community lined up in support of the evolutionary theory, students asserted the compatibility of science and faith. [89] Science and religion, it was held, had separate spheres. As long as each confined itself to its proper work—science to explain nature and religion to explain the spiritual and ethical dimensions of existence—there would be no conflict between the two. [90] As one student orator declared, "True science and true religion *cannot* be incompatible, and the controversy arises from each striving to do the work which properly belongs to the other." [91] The denial of any real incompatibility reveals how quickly and painlessly the new science was incorporated into an evangelical scheme.

The implication of Darwinism, as conceived by Oberlin students, was even more satisfactory and pleasing. Evolution, translated from biology to society, became moral progress. [92] Since Oberlin theology stressed the freedom of the will in seeking salvation, the idea of the possibility of human moral progress was congenial to it. As one student asserted, the new science could purify faith if "by its doctrine of evolution it can show that man, instead of being cursed with a nature irrevocably vicious, is endowed with a perpetual tendency to improvement."[93] The very possibility of the exercise of free will with its corollary of moral obligation was, perhaps, a result of evolution.[94] Thus were "natural selection" and the "struggle for survival" drained of those brutal and competitive implications which appealed to some secular and Christian thinkers and doers of the late nineteenth century, and used instead to support a belief in the ultimate governance of "love and truth."[95]

The advent of Darwinism at Oberlin contributed to two developments of great significance: a rebirth of science instruction and a transition in theology to the liberalism of Henry Churchill King.[96] The natural sciences expanded more rapidly than any other segment of the curriculum in the seventies and eighties. Oberlin, it was commonly believed, had been unreceptive to scientific studies in the past.[97] Although some scientific instruction had always been provided, philosophical, biblical, and language studies had been stressed.[98] Albert A. Wright, who became Professor of Geology and Natural History in 1874, was the Oberlin life scientist of the late nineteenth century. Trained for teaching in the old-fashioned way at a seminary with a brief postgraduate course in the sciences, he nevertheless accepted a version of evolution, including the theory of natural selection, and maintained that there was nothing in Darwinism incompatible with the essentials of Christianity.[99] The astonishing advances in scientific knowledge and technique, best illustrated by the evolutionary theory itself, required the adoption of an experimental method in science teaching. By the seventies, as other colleges and universities expanded their science offerings and provided more experimental work, an insistent student demand called for new-method science instruction at Oberlin. The lack of experimental laboratory work and the consequent superficiality of science instruction grieved many students. The editors of the *Oberlin Review* believed "this to be the greatest defect in the present college course, and we know that it keeps many men from our Scientific Department."[100] In 1876 Professor Wright offered in his course in zoology the "first systematic laboratory work of any sort which has been done in Oberlin College."[101] Laboratory techniques were adopted in chemistry in 1878 when a new teacher, William K. Kedzie, was appointed to the faculty.[102] One observer, confessing that Oberlin historically had been weak in the sciences, claimed that the new professors and new equipment made scientific instruction as good at Oberlin as anywhere.[103] President Fairchild, observing the rapid growth and new popularity of scientific instruction, was moved to reiterate his belief that philosophical studies should hold the pre-eminent place. The introduction of laboratory work and of advanced elective courses in chemistry, zoology, and geology, as well as

> the growing prominence of these studies in the world at large, are all influences that have tended to create a degree of interest in these branches among our students which we have not hitherto known. It will require all our diligence to retain for literary and philosophical studies their usual prominence. As yet there is probably no occasion for alarm.[104]

In the seventies and eighties the scientific subjects were invigorated and the foundations laid for a lasting tradition of sound scientific education.

Social science was another expanding field of study in the late nineteenth century. In academic popularity it gave way perhaps to the sciences and modern languages, but the differentiation and growth of social science subjects was one of the most important developments in higher learning. The content, of course, was not entirely novel. A limited study of current society, economics, and politics, largely from a philosophical and legalistic standpoint, had been included in the venerable course in Moral Philosophy, and in many colleges there were, as well, courses in political science and political economy.[105] Oberlin had long offered in both of these ways a commentary on contemporary society.[106] In 1842 Amasa Walker, a Massachusetts gentleman of independent means, who devoted himself to politics, reform causes, and the study of political economy, was appointed Professor of Political Economy and General History. He lectured at Oberlin from 1842 to 1850, resigning in order to accept election to the Massachusetts legislature.[107] After Walker's departure, the task of teaching political economy was passed from one member of the faculty to another.[108] When offered, the course consisted of a brief series of lectures during a single term with recitations from such texts as John Stuart Mill's *Political Economy,* Julian M. Sturtevant's *Economics,* and John M. Gregory's *New Political Economy.* The faculty acknowledged an obligation to provide some instruction in political economy, but the subject held at best only a third-class academic citizenship.

In the eighties adequate provision was first made for regular instruction in the social sciences. One of Oberlin's most illustrious alumni was James Monroe. As a young man, under the influence of William Lloyd Garrison, he had become a speaker for the abolitionist cause. Monroe entered Oberlin in 1844 to complete his education, graduating from the College in 1846 and from the theological seminary in 1849. While a student he supported himself by delivering antislavery lectures in Ohio towns. Although he was appointed professor of rhetoric and belles-lettres in 1849, much of his time was devoted to politics. In 1855 he was elected to the Ohio House of Representatives from Lorain County, serving until 1860. In that year he was elected to the Ohio Senate and was twice chosen president of that body. He resigned his seat in 1862 to accept an appointment from President Lincoln as United States consul in Rio de Janeiro. After his return to the United States, he served five successive terms as representative of Oberlin's congressional district in the national House of Representatives. Monroe was Oberlin's most eminent political figure, second only to Charles Grandison Finney as a public personage. After Finney's resignation in 1866, Monroe had declined the offer of the presidency of the College. He was a powerful speaker with great personal charm and firm Republican convictions.[109]

In 1880 President Fairchild announced that the College would establish a professorship in history and "possibly, too, a separate chair of Economics and Political Science."[110] Some of Monroe's friends, influential in college affairs, urged him to consider a position as professor of history and political science. They reminded him that his deep and varied political experience "at home and abroad will give to your teaching a richness and a value of no ordinary kind, and make your work a greatly useful one."[111] In 1882 these friends began to raise an endowment for a professorial chair. Within a year $35,000 in cash and good pledges had been secured, so the trustees appointed Monroe professor of political science and modern history.[112] After he began teaching in 1883, instruction in these subjects compared favorably with that in other academic disciplines.

Monroe's teaching consisted of lectures to seniors on political economy, modern history, and international law. His method included "recitations from approved text-books . . . supplemented by lectures and by applications of principles to existing institutions and current events."[113] He was the first history teacher at Oberlin to discuss modern times. Before his appointment Professor Judson Smith, most of whose teaching was in the theological seminary, had delivered a five-week course of lectures on "Modern History," beginning with the fall of the Roman Empire and originally brought down only to the early Norman kings of England, although Smith later added lectures on scholasticism and the Reformation. Monroe's lectures on modern history accorded better with current ideas of periodization since he began with the fall of Constantinople and brought the story of European history to the unification of Italy, including consideration of such topics and figures as Divine Providence and the Reformation, Louis XIV, and Frederick the Great. The course was largely organized around leading historical personages, a scheme which gave Monroe opportunities to exercise his oratorical talents.[114] He was one of the most popular Oberlin teachers of his day. His history classes were always large and students later recalled his lectures with pleasure.[115] According to a colleague, "he was a delightful gentleman and an able speaker. His lectures were full of illustrations drawn from his own experience. He was not exacting in his requirements but his students got a great deal that they could remember out of his courses."[116] Besides conducting the course in modern history, he delivered many public lectures on recent American events with which he had personal familiarity. Among these were accounts of John Brown's raid at Harper's Ferry, the disputed Hayes-Tilden presidential election, the abolitionist movement, and leading politicians and statesmen he had known in Congress and the diplomatic service.[117]

In his political economy courses Monroe taught the doctrines of classical, laissez-faire economics with the important exception of his advocacy of tariff protection.[118] Although the content of his teaching was familiar and conventional for the times, he was more of an innovator in method. An important service to Oberlin was the introduction of the seminar, which provided an opportunity for students with a special interest in political economy to investigate topics more thoroughly than would otherwise have been possible. In September, 1887, he organized a voluntary Political Economy Club which met weekly during the three terms of the school year. Each member prepared an essay on a current economic issue or a historical topic which was read at a club meeting and criticized by the other members and Professor Monroe. Very popular with students, the club numbered from thirty to as many as fifty members each term. Since its work was extracurricular, carrying no academic credit, the large numbers who joined indicate the enthusiasm and seriousness with which many students pursued the study of society and economics. A student writing in the *Oberlin Review* when the club was founded was confident that it would do its part in "preparing a generation of statesmen," by providing a place where "the great practical questions of the day" could be studied.[119] Among the members of the club who distinguished themselves later in life were John R. Commons, economist, labor historian, and social reformer at the University of Wisconsin; Guy S. Callender, pioneering economic historian at Yale University; and Glenn E. Plumb, labor lawyer and author of the Plumb plan for nationalizing the railroads after World War I. In 1894 the faculty approved the establishment of a seminar in political economy with full academic credit, thus ending the brief but successful career of the Political Economy Club.[120] Although Monroe was neither an original nor an acutely analytical economist, he introduced many students to current economic thinking and the study of economic and social problems. Few academic disciplines could equal the solid progress made in history and political economy under his guidance.

The greater prominence of the study of history and society in the curriculum corresponded to an increase among students in interest in social and economic issues. Both reflected an unease over injustices in American society and threats to social equilibrium.

With the strong tradition at Oberlin of concern over social questions, it is not startling that current social and political issues should have been popular subjects in literary society exercises and oratorical contests. Immediately after the close of the Civil War, however, most such student extracurricular efforts were vague and pointless. After all, with righteousness and nationalism apparently victorious in war, it was all too easy to glide into the comforting assumption that American life, now set in the right direction, was approaching perfection. It seemed unreasonable to suppose that the great sacrifices of the War were not matched by comparable gains, and so a mood of complacency settled over the attitudes and ideas about society held by many northern Protestants.[121]

This complacency was echoed by most Oberlin students. The strongest note in student social comment, and the assumption upon which nearly all of it rested, was that the nation and mankind faced the prospect of endless moral progress. In content, progress was usually identified with the spread of evangelical Protestantism and republican liberty. For example, in an oration entitled "Conscience in History," a student asserted that mankind's quest for a better life had culminated in nineteenth century America. The life of Christ, the Protestant Reformation, and the foundation of the American republic marked the great stages of humanity's advance.[122] Catchwords derived from the theory of evolution, faith in the power of Christianity, and the compelling example of American liberty were often combined as both historical explanation and prophecy. In an essay a student claimed that all social discontent would eventually disappear in the face of civil equality and the influence of Protestant Christianity. A universal social harmony would be established through "equality of human rights and uniformity of religious action." [123]

As the nineteenth century drew to a close this faith in sure and easy progress was called into question. That America was the vanguard of moral progress seemed beyond doubt, but disturbing evidence caused some to hesitate before reiterating their expectation of automatic improvement.[124] One student, for example, argued in a prize-winning oration that the principle of equal human rights, while never more fully honored than in his own day, was still very imperfectly realized:

> There lingers still among us, the most favored of the nations, distinctions and classes unworthy of free men. There is the tendency of wealth to arrogate to itself superiority. We have not all of us escaped from the prejudice that would despise a man for the color of his skin or the angle of his eye. . . . The man of toil does not yet receive for his labor that compensation which in justice belongs to him. There are thousands in our cities who are doomed to poverty and ignorance and misery by no fault of their own. Society lays upon their suffering shoulders its heaviest burdens, and requites their efforts with rags and crumbs, while its favorites revel in luxurious extravagance.[125]

An improvement in these conditions could be expected, but only with work and the passage of time. Such arguments testified to the beginnings of a breach in the wall of complacency.

The optimism of Oberlin students, then, began to be qualified by the discovery that serious challenges faced the United States, but they persisted in the belief that mild yet efficacious remedies were available to cure social and moral ills. The most dangerous challenge to social stability and justice, so they thought, was unrestricted immigration and its consequences. Almost without exception Oberlin students viewed immigrants with suspicion. The immigrant threatened the social progress, stability, and righteousness which, it had been assumed, would follow the great purgative of the Civil War. Unrestricted immigration, they argued, was the prime cause of many evils in American life and it had aggravated all the rest.[126] Massive immigration had undermined the effectiveness and equity of municipal government. In the competition for jobs, the immigrants drove down wages, creating poverty and unemployment for all. They corroded public morals, rejected sound religion, and strengthened the "liquor power." "Just as fast as the interests of temperance are advanced, the thousands of foreigners are on hand to degrade and lower public sentiment." [127] These fears were rooted in concern for the future of the Anglo-Saxon race. Its preservation, so they claimed, would serve the interests of all humanity: "Is it nothing to the world to preserve in all its pristine vigor the grand old Anglo-Saxon race? That race which has ever been foremost in the cause of liberty, which in ages past has continually scattered blessings to the nations as it has been steadily advancing along the highway of civilization." [128] The time required to absorb and Americanize the immigrants, so they thought, could be gained only through legal restriction. A few aliens might be safely allowed to enter: "They can fall in with the great American nation in its onward march, without a murmur of discontent along the lines, and instead of being a menace to our civilization, they will add strength and energy to our people, and, united in one grand homogeneous nation, we can work out the destiny of the world." [129]

Among the especially destructive effects of unrestricted immigration were the growing influence of Roman Catholicism and municipal political corruption. The immigrant masses, one student charged, were the "ready tools of usurping [Catholic] power."[130] Without restriction, immigration would finally destroy civil liberty and self-government.

With mass immigration seen as a threat to both established governmental and religious institutions, Americanism easily became identified with Protestantism. There had long been, of course, a disposition among many Protestants to forge the connection, but the immigration of the late nineteenth century confirmed the tendency.[131] At Oberlin, the principle of religious fellowship, while it prevented the development of some kinds of prejudice and exclusiveness, operated to exclude most of the immigrants. The "American way," on the other hand, defined as a set of specific allegiances, had little to attract those who found the allegiances alien and even meaningless. Rarely did a student favorably estimate the effects of immigration. An essay on the "Scandinavian in America," praised their literacy, industriousness, and piety.[132] Since the Scandinavians were Protestants and avoided the crowded cities in favor of farms and towns, there was little reason to fear their influence. Such appreciation sharply contrasted with the suspicion of other groups.

Poverty was a second major challenge to complacency. By the eighties the presence of a large working class, bound to a life of unrelieved toil and bare existence, was taken for granted. Orations and essays describing the harsh conditions of working-class life—the long hours of work, the low rates of pay, and the evils of the slum—were common in the late ninetenth century.[133] Literary societies frequently debated on some aspect of poverty. The stories and narrative poems of students were heavily laced with descriptions, sometimes sentimental, of the poor and their way of life.[134] Avarice, it was charged, dictated attitudes. It made employers look upon workers as machines instead of rational beings entitled to a wage sufficient to "live in comfort and some degree of refinement."[135] Echoing abolitionist rhetoric, one student declared: "Avarice . . . demands that a portion of the race be kept in virtual slavery in order that its coffers may be filled with the fruits of half-compensated toil."[136] If present trends continued, the "money power" would soon rule the nation and "when hard times come, the pent up wrath of years of oppression will burst forth and those ill gained treasures will be plundered by angry mobs."[137] Distributed as fair wages, however, the new wealth would inaugurate an unprecedented era of human progress. As earlier generations had won independence and destroyed slavery, so the present generation must take up "the yet grander work of emancipating human souls from the tyranny of avarice." [138] The embers of the abolitionist crusade helped to ignite the cause of social justice in an industrialized America.

The reluctance of the Protestant denominations to attack social injustice or to aid its victims was often condemned. Too many churchmen and churchgoers were complacent or hypocritical in the face of suffering and poverty. Too many wealthy urban congregations looked with indifference or even hostility upon the struggles of the underprivileged. One student, for example, contrasted the primitive Christian church, simple in worship and welcoming all classes of society, with a "Fifth Avenue Church" attended only by the wealthy. Because of the indifference of influential, wealthy congregations, many denominations failed to reach the lower classes, a failure which would eventually undermine Protestantism.[139]

Still there was no real consensus on the duty of the church to society. The proper relation between the church, with its religious objectives, and society, with its needs and moral deficiencies, was disputed. The fact that this issue arose testifies to the weakening hold of evangelicalism. The old contention that the only significant personal relation was that between the individual and God had its defenders. For the poor this offered inner regeneration and the hope of ultimate salvation while for the churches it suggested reliance upon standard evangelical methods. As one young woman wrote in an essay on tramps, the churches were the only agency working for "the reformation from the inside out of all classes." [140] Some students believed that the churches could best serve as a bulwark of existing society, in danger of destruction by an uprising from below. The evangelical churches should uplift and save the "haters of God and man" at the bottom of society lest they "prove . . . dangerous to national life." [141] On the other hand, some students were beginning to see the churches as an agent of social reform and the Christian faith as a manifesto of brotherhood. Many appeals for Christian leadership in social and economic reform were issued before the turn of the century.

Closely related to the spread of poverty was social disunity. American society was increasingly divided between the two destructive classes of "millionaires" and "anarchists," with the greed of the fortunate and the discontent of those below grinding "honest employers and faithful employes . . . between the upper and nether millstones of . . . industrial warfare." [142] Reforms, ameliorative and limited, aimed primarily at restoring an open society and the traditional harmonious relations between classes, were needed. Changes which would raise material standards of life for the poor merited support, but radical change, benefiting one class at the expense of others, was denounced.

The social thought of Oberlin students was meliorative and cautiously optimistic in outlook, derived from both a Christian concern for the fate of working people in an industrial, urban society and from a fear of triumphant radicalism unless social and economic changes were implemented. Raising wages, instituting profit-sharing plans, establishing co-operatives, even the organization of working men in trade unions, were the sort of specific remedies for social injustice that appealed to them.[143] Confidence in the power of Christian benevolence to solve social and economic problems marked the Oberlin reformer. As one student wrote, the difficulties of the age would be surmounted through "the spirit of volunteer service among the people, backed by an aggressive spirit of Christianity." [144]

Many opportunities for service were available. City missions attracted many alumni in training for the ministry.[145] The theological seminary maintained a Slavic Department which prepared ministers for work among the Slavic immigrants of the cities. Under its auspices seminary students conducted missions in the nearby cities of Cleveland and Lorain. The institutional church that provided religious, educational, recreational and civic services for its parishioners, was praised as the model for churches of the future.

New secular careers were available for those with the desire to serve. The city settlement houses, widely publicized in the nineties, provided an opportunity for Oberlin students to act upon their understanding of society's problems.[146] As an alumna settlement-house resident in New York put it: "The settlement stands between the ignorant rich and the ignorant poor, and when it has brought these two classes to a mutual understanding of their needs, hindrances, and resources, its work will be done." The settlement house allayed suspicions and harmonized the interests of social classes. It aimed "to represent America to an immigrant population that knows nothing of our language, customs, laws and is scandalously imposed upon as a consequence. . . . To bring about a mutual understanding between rich and poor. . . . To help our young neighbors as we would our own younger brothers and sisters."[147] A movement which accorded so neatly with the fears and hopes of Oberlin students was enthusiastically supported.[148]

One current of student social thought ran deeper. A few believed that injustice required more drastic measures than settlement houses or institutional churches. Their reforming spirit also sprang from their religious faith, but it had a cutting edge and a sense of urgency lacking in the concern for social injustice shown by most students.

The best-known member of this group, both at Oberlin and later, was John Rogers Commons, who came under the influence of Henry George's ideas while still a student. Partially supported by his mother, who moved to Oberlin and operated a student boarding house while her children were in college, Commons became a resourceful student, participant in local reform movements, accomplished public speaker, and editor of the student newspaper.[149] The source of his early interest in reform was his Christian faith. In an article entitled "Our Civilization," published at the close of his senior year, he argued that the Christian religion since its foundation had been at work to better the world: "Christianity has been no dainty reformer, fearing contamination, but has boldly attacked every relation of society. Conquering often, often defeated, it has made the history of civilization the history of the Christian religion."[150] The time had arrived, he thought, to resort once again to the example of the faultless life of Jesus as the inspiration for a new era of reform.

Commons chided students who became preoccupied with private concerns and lost all interest in the lives of others. In an editorial called "Abstract Studies and the World," he warned against the isolation of the educated person from the masses. Complacent isolation was a "danger peculiar to students . . . under the influence of abstract studies and intellectual aims."[151] Because of it, "we are apt to lose or fail to gain a living interest in the great working classes of our country, and a sympathy for those whom we are said to have always with us, the poor." He detested the sentimental sympathy conventionally expressed by some students which produced no discernible results. "There is, indeed, a maudlin sympathy cropped from books, which adorns essays and orations, or serves as a dialectic thrust in society debates, but that it takes practical hold on the heart is to be doubted." The prohibitionists, he thought, sometimes yielded to the temptation to pursue moral abstractions at the expense of real helpfulness. Student discussions and writings on conditions among the poor were too often superficial and unrealistic. They sometimes seemed to be no more than gestures:

> How many of us think of putting ourselves in the place of the working-man and realizing how we should do under his circumstances? Perhaps he is suffering great injustice, and certainly the signs indicate that our social machine is somewhere badly out of gear, but how are we to find where the wrong is or intelligently look for a remedy, if, in our theories and abstractions, we are wafted out of contact with those whose lives and homes are most desperately at stake?

The duty of educated men did not lie in formulating soul-satisfying abstractions nor in aspiring to an aristocracy of intellect but in serving as guides "whom the army of the discontented may trust and follow."[152] Much of Commons' later career as reformer, author, and teacher consisted of ideas and actions grounded upon these premises.

In 1882 Commons had read Henry George's *Progress and Poverty*.[153] Like so many other reformers of his generation he was moved by the sincerity and force of George's protest against social inequities. George's ideas were discussed more frequently at Oberlin in the eighties than those of any other social critic. Questions of taxation of land values and of private versus public ownership of land became subjects of regular debate in the literary societies.[154] A student group arranged to bring Henry George to Oberlin in March, 1887, for an address entitled "Land and Labor." The newspaper devoted most of its editorial space to a review and appreciation of his remarks in the issue following the lecture, which was in itself a mark of regard for the speaker and an indication of unusual student interest in the subject. The editors praised his skillful oratory, and his courtesy in answering "every question without evasion and with commendable gentlemanliness." As he explained his doctrines, they seemed "much less revolutionary than was supposed."[155]

The lecture stirred great interest. Following his appearance his ideas were debated in all of the literary societies. The *Oberlin Review* reported that "the most exciting and interesting general debate this term was on the Henry George land tax question." [156] A few students announced their conversion to the single tax. A Henry George Club, small and short-lived, was organized by Commons and some of his friends. It was the first Oberlin student association dedicated to a particular social reform since ante bellum times. The first meeting of the club, on December 17, 1887, was held in "Mr. Commons' Room, Main St.," where he presided over a meeting of nine disciples. The constitution of the club, eventually signed by eleven students, proclaimed its object to be "to investigate, discuss and promulgate the Tax Reform proposed by Mr. George." [157] The Club held six meetings between December, 1887, and February, 1888. The meeting of January 20, for example, opened with prayer, following which, "Pres[ident] Commons read . . . a brief statem[en]t of [the] law of rent and 7 deductions therefrom concisely giving [the] Geo[rge] doct[rine] in a nut-shell. Mr. Weld then opened a discussion of [the] quest[io]n how improvem[en]ts can be distinguished fr[om] land." At subsequent meetings the members discussed such topics as the analogy between rent and interest and George's contention that industrial depressions were caused by private ownership of land. The Oberlin Henry George Club soon expired, the victim, probably, of the approach of college examinations and the end of the school year.

Commons and his friends carried George's ideas into the classroom. For Professor James Monroe's Political Economy Club, Commons wrote a paper on "The Principles of Taxation," in which he drew upon George's writings for criticisms of orthodox economists.[158] Commons and Harold A. Weld received permission to lecture to Monroe's class in beginning political economy on George's ideas during four class sessions. As Commons later wrote: "Harry took the deductive God-given rights of man to the land. I took the statistics . . . It was all directly contrary to our Professor's Republican party and protectionism." [159] Monroe encouraged the young economists to continue their investigations.

After Commons' graduation in 1888 George's theories continued to attract attention and a following. In the nineties debates on such topics as "should taxes be on land values only?" and "resolved, that the single tax theory is inferior to our present system," were frequent in the literary societies.[160] Professor Monroe critically examined

George's ideas in classroom and public lectures.[161] Edward B. Haskell, one of the members of the club, became George's principal Oberlin champion. His seminary commencement oration in 1891 was entitled "The Religious Side of the Land Question." According to the *Oberlin Review* he boldly claimed that "the system which Henry George advocates was first laid down in the Mosaic law. The oration was . . . a plea for the Single Tax System, with the provision that if this were not the best way to rectify our present system we should be governed by benevolence in whatever method we adopt."[162] Apparently he doubted the likelihood of an immediate trial of the single tax.

At Oberlin, as elsewhere, the writings of Henry George were more of an inspiration than a blueprint for reform. His indictment of industrial society and his plea for social justice were more influential than his specific proposals. The George movement, including only a few students, marked the limit of enthusiasm for social reform.[163] Despite attempts to moderate the meaning of his ideas, his theories were still too sweeping and his remedies too extreme to attract much student support.

In the eighties Oberlin students experienced a social awakening. Literary society and oratorical contest programs became so laden with discussions of current political, social, and economic controversies, that the failure to include any orations on such matters in the Home Oratorical Contest of 1887 was thought notable and refreshing.[164] The students led the way toward new thinking about society and toward new forms of service. They inherited and transmitted Oberlin's social conscience. President Fairchild, on those rare occasions when he addressed himself to social problems, denied that there was a deep conflict between capital and labor. Accordingly, he relied upon the slow improvement of individual character as the means of reconciliation and social salvation.[165] "Rude and unsatisfactory as [the present division of wealth] is," he wrote, "society can be made very comfortable and prosperous, with an abundant application on every side of the ethical principles of neighborly forbearance and good-will."[166] Probably all Oberlin students would have agreed that the reformation of character was indispensable in the work of social reform. The continuing support for the temperance and prohibition causes as means of social reform testifies to the strong appeal of character reformation to the students of the time. But the articulate students were not willing to rely entirely upon character reformation in seeking a just society, whether employed through direct appeals or by way of the inspirational example. Defects of character and training were important but they could not account for social strife and injustice in all their complexity. The social machine was out of gear, and the causes lay in part in impersonal, and still rather mysterious, factors.

The fact that students had started to grope for answers to social questions was, after all, of the greatest significance. They acknowledged their need for more accurate information and more penetrating theories about society as the complexities of modern social life impinged upon their awareness. So, as Oberlin's social conscience was reborn and found expression in social service, it produced a demand for less superficial instruction in the workings of society. The old course in Moral Philosophy with its collection of generalities on formal and legal aspects of society and the one-term course of lectures on political economy intermittently offered to seniors did not suffice in the new age. In the eighties Oberlin undertook to offer regular and systematic instruction in those subjects which were becoming the social sciences. During the nineties, a succession of young, university-trained teachers led the social sciences to first-class academic status. The advent of social reform and a more careful study of society interlocked in a mutually beneficial relationship. Trained intelligence assumed a share in the work of reform with the soul kindled by love of God and pity of man.

If this new interest in more advanced study was to be satisfied, there was a great need for scholarly materials and aids. Laboratories and their apparatus were being provided for the sciences. For other disciplines, books were the tools of the trade. As long as simple textbook recitation was the method of classroom procedure, there was little need to consult library books. Only students driven by curiosity or those preparing society exercises needed to enter the library, which was consequently neglected in the college budget. In 1874 the collection amounted to only 9,400 volumes, supplemented by 2,900 volumes in the library of the literary societies.[167] The accommodations of the library were not designed to facilitate access to books. The space was inadequate, with few shelves for books and few chairs for students. The librarian, a retired minister, commanded only a small salary and appropriately kept the library open only a few hours each day. The college collection largely consisted of seldom read theological works. Most were of no use to students.[168] The literary societies' collection, which doubtless reflected student interests more accurately, consisted of works of fiction, poetry, history, biography, philosophy, and literary criticism. These books were grist for the society exercise mill. In 1879, it was said that *"Paradise Lost* . . . enjoys the highest honors of the library," with the poems of Longfellow and Tennyson not far behind. In the history section the first volumes of numerous sets were "ragged or rebound" while remaining volumes were in new condition, "bearing witness alike to the ambition and inconstancy of the student."[169] In the eighties the library began to receive recognition as a means of study and scholarship. Recent scholarly works as well as classics were added in considerable numbers. By 1889 the library contained 36,000 volumes. The number of books drawn, and the use of books for collateral reading in courses, had increased many times over in a few years.[170] With the construction of the Spear Library the shortage of space was relieved, and with the appointment of Azariah S. Root as librarian in 1887, the building of a first-rate college collection was launched.[171] The changing character of the library, the curriculum, and the faculty revealed an acceptance of a more profound and independent scholarship as the main goal of an institution of learning.

By the late eighties some of the younger alumni as well as students and some faculty believed that the College was failing to meet all the needs of the age. Oberlin's tone and teaching they thought were narrow and parochial; improvements, they hinted, could not be expected until there was an infusion of new blood.[172] Others believed that an outmoded curriculum was the major defect.[173] One Oberlin professor wrote in his journal in 1887: "All accounts agree that alumni are quite dissatisfied with our course of study and methods of teaching."[174] A movement for reform began in 1887 when a Minneapolis, Saint Paul, and Chicago group issued a call for an alumni convention to meet in Chicago in July.[175] A committee consisting of Merritt Starr of Chicago and George H. Mead and Norman P. Willard of Minneapolis planned the meeting. The faculty appointed President Fairchild, Mrs. Johnston, John M. Ellis, Henry

C. King, and Lyman B. Hall as their representatives.[176] The opening address, by Philip C. Hayes of Morris, Illinois, was a blueprint for a new Oberlin consisting of "a great University . . . [a] New $5000 President . . . and Election of Trustees by Alumni," all of which Professor Hall thought "very radical."[177] Hayes proposed the addition of many new courses in different disciplines, the abolition of the Greek and Latin requirements, a campaign to raise $100,000 to endow the presidency, and the direct election by the alumni of two members of the board of trustees each year.[178] There is little doubt that the alumni who called the convention wanted to suggest retirement to President Fairchild, then seventy years of age, and to raise obstacles to the election of Professor Ellis as Fairchild's successor.[179] In later sessions the faculty representatives reminded the alumni of the great material and academic progress that had been made in recent years.[180]

Certainly there had been substantial progress, but change had come too slowly to suit many students and alumni. During Fairchild's administration many important issues were raised but not fully resolved. The fabric of college religious life was still outwardly intact, but some evangelical practices now seemed excessive, revivals were not so frequent, and piety was not so demonstrative as it once had been. The substitution in 1874 of lectures on secular subjects for the sermon at the Thursday lecture was the only change made in religious services or requirements while Fairchild was president.[181] The steady decline in the number of Oberlin graduates entering the ministry was perhaps a better indication of the weakening of the old evangelicalism, although in part this decline also reflected a conviction among students that vocations besides the ministry offered good opportunities for service to God and man.[182] Still, the guardians of the evangelical tradition were alarmed. The readiness in the near future to abandon many of the old forms of piety best reveals their loose hold on the students of Fairchild's day. The conviction that education should be founded upon faith was in transition.

By 1889 the old curriculum and teaching methods had been shaken by the realization that truth was an elusive quarry. It could no longer be confidently assumed that the truth, whole and rightly proportioned, was known, needing only to be handed on to the next generation. Instead, truth had to be discovered; it was the object of a continuing quest for the ideas that would explain and master reality. As students and teachers moved toward a critical conception of knowledge, they added an element of intellectuality to the Oberlin enterprise. Oberlin, as one perceptive student wrote, had undergone "a wide awakening" during the eighties, evidenced in better methods of teaching, stricter academic requirements, and "the enthusiastic spirit of scholarship." Its task now, he continued, was to push ahead "to the front rank of scholarship and learning, always guided by the early spirit of moral and religious training." [183]

## CHAPTER III

# BUILDING THE NEW OBERLIN

The nineties were trying years for Oberlin as they were for the United States. Severe depression, social conflict, Populism, the battle of the standards, and imperialistic war agitated the nation. Oberlin confronted less hazardous but still important challenges. New concepts of truth and the means of its discovery, with appropriate new academic methods, had been foreshadowed. However, no settled consensus had been reached on the question, fundamental for Oberlin, of the relationship between religion and learning. In the nineties, issues were brought into sharper relief under the impact of changing leadership, ambitious schemes for expansion, and a financial crisis. The result was a period of instability lasting until the very close of the decade when a new order began to emerge.

Unsteadiness characterized the college presidency, the highest level of leadership. Oberlin had only three presidents in the fifty-six years before 1889; this continuity was disrupted during the nineties. For two relatively long and harmful periods, from 1889 to 1891 and from 1896 to 1898, Oberlin had no president. The prolonged consideration of the succession problem in each instance led to the formation of factions among faculty, trustees, and alumni, each pressing its own solution. These circumstances tended to accentuate divisions.

The question of succession arose in June, 1889, with the resignation of President Fairchild. In his opinion, and in that of most of the older members of the faculty, the board, and the Oberlin constituency of alumni and friends, the heir should be Professor John M. Ellis.[1] This large and influential group feared for the College if Ellis were not selected. Samuel F. Cooper, a trustee, expressed their attitude when he wrote to Fairchild: "I look with concern upon the indications of a movement particularly among the later alumni, to change the nature of the College so that eventually not a vestage [sic] of *our* Oberlin, the real Oberlin will be left, only her skeleton dressed in the borrowed clothes of a modern University." Cooper, afraid that the board would not elect Ellis, suggested that Fairchild remain in office as president emeritus with Ellis appointed acting president.[2] Another candidate, acceptable to many of the same people, was Judson Smith, secretary of the American Board of Commissioners of Foreign Missions. Smith, although a graduate of Amherst College, had received most of his undergraduate training at Oberlin and he had returned to study in the theological seminary and, later, to teach. As Charles C. Creegan, an alumnus, wrote to Fairchild, Smith would "make an earnest effort to hold the institution to all that is essentially Oberlin." Creegan feared that others who were being considered, especially those without a prior association with Oberlin, would fail to perpetuate the spirit of the old College.[3]

Three faculty members—Ellis, Henry C. King, associate professor of mathematics, and William G. Ballantine, professor of Old Testament language and literature in the theological seminary—were given serious consideration in 1889. A majority of the faculty supported King, although, according to one professor, with little enthusiasm. Unknown, youthful, and inexperienced, he was unacceptable to some trustees.[4] Another possibility was John G. W. Cowles, a Cleveland banker, member of a pioneer Oberlin family, and a trustee, but he declined to take office unless elected unanimously.[5]

Once the local candidates had been considered, those trustees and alumni who preferred someone from outside Oberlin were given an opportunity to make nominations. They believed the College needed new blood. Although there was some vagueness in their formula, they hoped the new president would be an experienced executive, receptive to both educational innovations and a measured religious liberalism, and would possess a national reputation as an educator. Trustees Lucien C. Warner, Michael Strieby, and Amzi Barber approached and eventually offered the position to Merrill T. Gates, the layman president of Rutgers College.[6] Gates waited two months to decline, choosing instead to accept the presidency of Amherst College. His decision relieved the many Oberlin alumni who considered his election a dangerous move toward a liberal, secular, and easternized Oberlin.[7] At Amherst, with revealing irony, he provoked controversy as an anachronistic champion of aggressive evangelicalism.[8]

When the board and faculty returned to home ground, they finally —and unanimously—elected William Gay Ballantine.[9] "At Chapel he was greeted with wild enthusiasm by the students with [the] College yell and the various class yells in succession [,] waving of handkerchiefs etc. . . . Pres[ident] Ballantine made a wonderfully happy speech."[10] Seemingly the great matter was resolved and a painful period ended. The election of Ballantine was a compromise. He was not a representative of old Oberlin like John Ellis, since he had received no part of his education there, a desideratum of the conservatives. He had, however, received his undergraduate degree from Marietta, an Ohio college much like Oberlin.[11] Following preparation for college teaching at Union Theological Seminary in New York City, he taught Greek and Hebrew at Ripon College and later at Indiana University. In 1878 he came to the Oberlin theological seminary as professor of Old Testament language and literature. His service as chairman of the faculty in the period between Fairchild's resignation and his own election to the presidency afforded some administrative experience. As for other qualifications for the presidency, he enjoyed a local reputation as a scholar, had an extensive and exact knowledge of Hebrew, and was an effective teacher. Although he held no advanced academic degree, he could plausibly represent the scholarly aspirations of some Oberlin faculty members. Those who hoped that Oberlin would obtain a president of national reputation could only be disappointed as he neither wrote books nor made public addresses. The first choice of few, he was acceptable as a second choice to many.

Ballantine's inaugural address, delivered on July 1, 1891, reflected the circumstances of his election. He tried to combine old and new, assuring Oberlinians that they need fear no startling innovations during his regime, but also claiming that some changes were desirable.[12] The address began and ended with praise of the evangelical college. Oberlin, he said, had never fallen into the error of asserting that the primary purpose of college study was the training of the intellect. The Oberlin ideal was the development of the student's entire character and potentiality, morally and religiously as well as intellectually.[13] The "supreme concern" of the College "had been and should continue to be the Education of the will—the complete subjugation of it to conscience." Liberal education without religious instruction was absurd and inconceivable. "The college of liberal arts must be saturated with religion." The faculty bore a heavy responsibility in this respect: "The student's conversion should stand first in the solicitude of his teachers." Regardless of new academic fashions, a teacher should not present all sides of a question with "equal candor and equal indifference," leaving the student to make an unguided choice. This procedure would teach the student "to regard indifference as mature and wise." The object of education was to prepare for practical life, which required a readiness to decide and act, as well as to know. "A learned man without courage in confession, decision in action, and enthusiasm in defense of truth is utterly unfit for a teacher of youth, for he misrepresents the very purpose of education." [14]

With these reassurances, Ballantine combined certain departures from tradition. The development of the whole man had been slighted by the colleges. The ideal academic training should provide a taste of every subject. The variety of college studies should not be limited on the false theory that proficiency in one field guaranteed proficiency in all. The ideal youth must undertake many studies—sciences, languages, social sciences, philosophy, psychology, ethics, theology, art, and even athletics—or risk irreparable intellectual and moral loss. Ballantine favored a great enlargement of elective courses for the odd reason that "a large percentage of mankind must, for various reasons, accept an education somewhat less than liberal," and should therefore be given an opportunity to specialize.[15] His insistence that the curriculum should be both broader and deeper implied expansion at Oberlin since some of the subjects he cited as necessary for liberal and special training were being taught either not at all or only in introductory courses. The address promised fundamental adherence to the old evangelicalism with significant additions in academic fields and offerings. It contained something for everyone.

The other addresses delivered at the inauguration reveal the hopes and fears of students, alumni, and faculty at this juncture.[16] Two speakers, Robert A. Millikan and Amzi Barber, a student and a trustee respectively, looked to the future in anticipation of its opportunities. Millikan, a member of the class of 1891, expressed advanced student opinion in calling for substantial academic reform.

The College, he thought, stood "upon the threshhold of a new era; . . . the new administration has possibilities before it which its predecessors never saw." The students, while rejoicing in the great academic progress that had been made in the past half dozen years, considered it only a beginning. Changing times required new endeavors and emphases, implying not a repudiation but a fulfillment of the meaning of Oberlin's history.

> We have no idle regrets to offer because Oberlin is changing. We live in different times and under other circumstances than did those true men, the Oberlin pioneers. . . . We should imitate them in all that made them great, in their sincerity; but we cannot, if we would, imitate them in all their ways and methods. . . . If we, in the different days we live in and the different paths we follow are but as earnest, as sincere men as they were, if our actions square as well with our convictions as theirs did, we shall be their worthy imitators.[17]

Fidelity to the past required progress, not simple imitation. Millikan suggested three major lines of development: the endowment should be increased, a proposal to which few could take exception; the course of study should be broadened; and, more controversially, the College should acquire "university facilities."[18] Three other speakers, Rev. Dan F. Bradley, Mrs. Martha Kincaid, and Rev. B. A. Imes, all alumni, laid great emphasis upon the importance of continuity. As Mrs. Kincaid expressed their thought, Oberlin should "take her stand on the impregnable rock of the Holy Scriptures," preparing students for useful service in the world, not for a limitless "cramming" of knowledge.[19]

Professor Henry C. King delivered a long address on behalf of the faculty, invoking the Oberlin past as the best guide to the future. Oberlin, he said, was a college that "*stands for something,*" one with definite ideals, aims, and principles of its own, "which is not striving to be a second anything else." It stood for democracy which King defined as the absence of special privilege. The College was morally and historically opposed to "the aristocracy of color, the aristocracy of sex, the aristocracy of wealth, the aristocracy of cliques, and the aristocracy of mere intellectual brilliancy."[20] King thus aligned himself with those who refused to sacrifice the historic College to alien ideals. The overriding purpose of Oberlin was the cultivation of

Christian character which should be pursued "not apologetically, but confessedly, avowedly, aggressively, unhesitatingly, on a religious and a Christian foundation." [21] In speaking of the faculty, King congratulated Ballantine and Oberlin for possessing teachers diverse in temperament and training. Despite differences over means the faculty was blessed with a genuine harmony in respect to ends.

King's address closed with a statement of aims for each academic department, which showed his determination to make a place for a sound scholarship in the service of religious goals. Each department's work ought to be grounded in a Christian conception of the universe. The department of history, for example, would be "impartial, accurate, painstaking in research and induction," but it would "not mock a unity seeking mind with mere bundles of labelled facts, without unity, without interpretation . . . without evolving plan, without end." [22] It would "see God in history, and . . . recognize an end great enough to justify the cost of centuries." [23] The department of political science would "not assume selfishness as its one guiding star; but, willing to blink no hardest fact," would still believe "in the possibility of the application of the ethics of Christ to every social problem, and with patient, assiduous study and toil," would seek "to evoke personal devotion to this test of the twentieth century." [24] The department of natural science would observe, experiment, generalize, and classify nature but it would remember that "underneath all science there must lie a metaphysics quite other than the shallow empiricism of the unthinking mind," and that "human nature is a part of nature, and that the ideal has its claims, and will not suffer the atrophy of the best in man." [25] For philosophy, his own subject, he pledged a due recognition of the new science of experimental psychology but insisted that a "philosophy or theory of life which dries the fountains of emotion, paralyzes thought and withers will at its inception, has no claim to urge at the bar of reason." [26] The College was justified both religiously and socially in its effort to encourage personal commitment to the Christian faith because, apart from the ultimate destination of the student's soul, it was only through such commitment that destructive tendencies in American life, such as the absence of serious intellectual endeavor, the desire for material comfort, and the fragmentation of interests, could be counteracted.[27] However, the old passion for doing the Lord's work had to be refined by a willingness to face facts and pursue knowledge with an equal ardor.

The delivery of this address by Professor King was a token of his emergence as the leading member of the faculty. The resignation of President Fairchild in 1889, followed in a few years by the death of Professor Ellis and the retirement of Professor Monroe, marked the transmission of power and office to a new generation. King's qualifications for leadership rested upon his formal training, long association with the College, and theological interests and skill. His father, Henry Jarvis King, enrolled at Oberlin in 1851 to prepare for the ministry but withdrew before graduation to become an official of Hillsdale College in Michigan, where Henry Churchill King was born and received his early education. In his sophomore year, he transferred from Hillsdale to Oberlin. While a student he participated in religious organizations and a literary society, and was editor of the *Oberlin Review*. Entering the Oberlin theological seminary in 1879, he decided upon a career in teaching after long consideration of the foreign mission field. Studies in theology, philosophy, and mathematics at Harvard University followed, and he received the Master of Arts degree in 1884. In the same year he was appointed associate professor of mathematics at Oberlin, a subject he taught until the early nineties when he gradually shifted into philosophy and theology. He drained the college philosophy courses of obtrusive indoctrination, greatly expanded the offerings of the Philosophy Department, and introduced more critical methods of inquiry and teaching, while firmly grounding the department's work on a Christian metaphysics. His formal philosophical and theological training was completed in 1893–94 at the University of Berlin in study with the liberal theologians Julius Kaftan, Otto Pfleiderer, and Adolf von Harnack.[28]

King's systematic theological work, the fruit of his reading and teaching in the 1890's, is contained in two volumes. *Reconstruction in Theology*, an elaboration of his inaugural lecture as professor of theology, presented his statement of theological principles.[29] In it he dealt with the pressing questions for theology which arose from developments in other spheres of thought. His second major book, *Theology and the Social Consciousness: A Study of the Relations of the Social Consciousness to Theology*, grew out of a course of lectures delivered at the Harvard Summer School of Theology in 1901.[30]

King wrote and spoke voluminously, but almost without exception his later writings applied the principles developed in these two books to particular problems and situations.[31] His goal always was to state theological principles which could be used by college students in answering the practical questions of life. Neither of the two works presented a complete system of theology. Instead they represented the more limited attempt to confront problems for theology that had recently arisen in science and biblical criticism and to point the direction that theology should take in solving them.

The task of the Christian theologian was a conservative one: he must "make real to his own generation the great abiding truths of Christianity."[32] But theology was not a static science, immutably fixed by the great system-makers of the past. The full meaning of God's revelation to man came only with the passage of time, so the need to assess and interpret revelation was never completely satisfied. In *Reconstruction in Theology* King restated the fundamental Christian conception of a personal God, who, through Christ, could be known by men and could influence their lives. Just when much of human life was becoming depersonalized through being enmeshed in immense, intricate organizations, he reaffirmed faith in a vital, personal God and reaffirmed the worth of individual personality. The "New Theology" of advanced liberals, resting upon a conception of God as strictly immanent in nature and history, led to a pantheism in which God, ceasing to be distinct, was merged with impersonal, although it was sanguinely believed, benevolent processes. If this conception were to rule theological thinking unchallenged, the personal God of traditional Christianity might well disappear entirely from human thought. King tried to bridge the gap that had opened between the traditional conception of a personal God and the new idea of a God at work with man to better the world. By emphasizing the persons of God and Christ, instead of God's immanence in nature and society, King's faith was partially protected from damage through reverses in human endeavor. The duty of improving the world, voluntarily assumed, rested primarily upon men; moral and social progress would not come automatically through divine immanence.

Much of the need for a reconstruction in theology derived from the extraordinary success and prestige of scientific method. King's analysis of the relationship between science and theology set sharp

limits for both. The scientists dealt with questions of fact and immediate cause; ultimate questions of meaning and destiny were within the province of the theologian, the religious philosopher, and of
all men when they thought upon religion. There was, he believed,
no irreconcilable conflict between science and religion. They were
directly concerned with different things. Only when they stepped
outside their proper boundaries could conflicts occur. The scientist
was utterly free to pursue facts and trace immediate causes. Freedom
of investigation meant that "all questions as to the conditions of the
appearance of life, of man, of conscience; and all questions of the
method of God's historical self-revelation . . . are to be freely and
fearlessly investigated in the most strictly scientific way."[33] Both the
theory of the evolution of life, as the best scientific hypothesis, and
unhampered critical analysis of the Bible, hopefully leading to a
more precise knowledge of God's will, could be accepted without
sacrifice of essential Christian beliefs.[34] At the same time, however,
King held to the possibility of the literal truthfulness of New Testament accounts of miracles by attempting to distinguish between the
universality and the uniformity of law. Although law was universal,
man's understanding of it was imperfect, so it might not always seem
to be uniform. Miracles might occur as a direct result of God's love
for man.[35]

King's accommodation of religion with the evolutionary idea and
scientific biblical criticism was offered to Oberlin students beginning
in the late 1880's. In his Bible classes and after 1890 in the courses
of the Philosophy Department, in particular the course devoted to the
study of the Microcosmus of the German philosopher Hermann
Lotze, from which the mediation between science and religion was
drawn, he attempted to provide a new foundation for faith.[36]

The election of President Ballantine proved to be only a temporary
solution to the problem of leadership. Respected as a scholar and
teacher, he was only tolerated as a leader. His failure to solve the
difficult financial problems facing Oberlin, which stemmed largely
from the depression of the nineties, frustrated the hopes of some
faculty and alumni by preventing the execution of ambitious plans
for expansion and even threatened to force a contraction of Oberlin's
instructional work and faculty. Declining enrollment, low salaries,
faculty resignations, and a series of budget deficits all contributed to

a loss of confidence which led him to submit his resignation in June, 1896.[37]

Given the problems that were left unsolved by the Ballantine regime, the search for a successor was bound to be difficult. A number of candidates were considered and again, as in 1891, one was chosen only to decline to accept the position. Only Professor King among faculty members was given serious consideration. The faculty hoped King would be offered the presidency, but the trustees refused to elect him. The trustees agreed that the new president should possess "spiritual power," "personal magnetism," intellectual vigor, and great executive ability.[38] They wanted a president with prestige and influence who could effectively represent the College to the public.

In November, 1898, Rev. John Henry Barrows, pastor of the First Presbyterian Church in Chicago for fifteen years, was elected to the presidency.[39] His skill as an executive had been demonstrated by his chairmanship of the Committee on Religious Congresses, which had organized the World's Parliament of Religions as part of the World's Columbian Exposition at Chicago in 1893. Although an influential churchman with an engaging, urbane personality and master of a popular style of oratory, he was neither a scholar nor an experienced academic administrator.[40] His achievements during four years as president of Oberlin lay in the realms of outside representation and finance. Thanks to his labors and an improving national economy, the College emerged from its crippling financial slump. Barrows' greatest success was the planning and execution of a campaign to raise $500,000 for endowment. In addition, large gifts were received for several needed buildings and other special purposes.

Academic decisions were left almost entirely in the hands of the faculty. Professor King was appointed Dean of the College in 1901 and authorized to superintend the formulation of academic policy. Barrows, insofar as he made pronouncements on academic questions, confined himself to praise of traditional Oberlin. In his inaugural address, entitled "The Ideals of Christian Education: The Argument for the Christian College," he presented a historical survey of Oberlin and reiterated his allegiance to the specific aims of the Christian college.[41] However necessary additional material resources, no amount of new funds, buildings, teachers, and equipment could replace the self-sacrificing spirit of serving God and mankind. Unlike some,

Barrows did not fear that greater wealth would undermine the College's traditional loyalties. As he reassuringly wrote: "I believe with all my heart that the Oberlin spirit is as active today in the College life as ever before, and with increased facilities and augmented energies, which can be furnished only by larger resources, I am confident that the old spirit of devotion to truth and humanity will still be controlling." [42] Barrows' tolerance and his willingness to permit others to exercise decisive influence in the academic, religious, and social life of the College opened the way for substantial changes during his presidency. Although his time in office, like Ballantine's, was brief, it did usher in a period of stable leadership. By the time of Barrows' unexpected death in 1902, Professor Henry C. King was judged ready to assume the presidency, which he held for twenty-five years, the longest term in Oberlin's history.

The Oberlin faculty in the nineties was even more unstable and more altered than the presidency. The decade was unparalleled in the rapid turnover of teachers. The following table shows the number of faculty members and their education between the academic years 1891–92 and 1901–2.[43] Of the nineteen faculty members of 1891–92, only six were still teaching at Oberlin in 1901–2.[44] Thus 70 per cent of the twenty teachers in 1901–2 had been appointed within the preceding ten years. In the same period a total of fifty persons served on the college faculty. The number of faculty members who were educated in whole or in part at Oberlin steadily declined. In 1891–92, 74 per cent had received at least part of their collegiate training at Oberlin. By 1901–2 this figure had dropped to 35 per cent. The Oberlin faculty of 1901–2 was a far more heterogeneous body than it had ever been before.[45]

The academic preparation of the faculty had significantly improved (see tabulation on page 80). The College responded to the demand for teachers specially prepared by advanced work to teach particular subjects. By the close of this period the seminary-trained clergyman-teacher was recognized as an anachronism. Ten of the faculty members of 1891–92, slightly more than half, were graduates of theological seminaries, but only four were in 1901–2.[46] In 1891–92 only 42 per cent of the Oberlin faculty had earned an advanced degree in an academic discipline and only one member of the faculty held an earned doctorate, although some of the faculty members who had

## Oberlin College Faculty, 1891–1902

| Year | Total Faculty | Held at Least One Oberlin Degree | Educated Entirely at Oberlin | Educated Entirely Elsewhere | Earned Degree in a Discipline | Earned Ph.D. | New Faculty Members | Left by End of Year |
|---|---|---|---|---|---|---|---|---|
| 1891–1892 | 19 | 14 | 6 | 5 | 8 | 1 | 2 | 4 |
| 1892–1893 | 19 | 12 | 5 | 7 | 10 | 3 | 4 | 3 |
| 1893–1894 | 22 | 11 | 5 | 11 | 13 | 3 | 6 | 4 |
| 1894–1895 | 21 | 9 | 3 | 12 | 13 | 3 | 3 | 3 |
| 1895–1896 | 18 | 9 | 3 | 9 | 11 | 2 | — | 1 |
| 1896–1897 | 18 | 9 | 3 | 9 | 12 | 2 | 1 | 2 |
| 1897–1898 | 20 | 8 | 4 | 12 | 16 | 4 | 4 | 3 |
| 1898–1899 | 21 | 9 | 3 | 12 | 16 | 5 | 4 | 3 |
| 1899–1900 | 23 | 9 | 3 | 14 | 18 | 6 | 5 | 5 |
| 1900–1901 | 22 | 8 | 3 | 14 | 17 | 7 | 4 | 2 |
| 1901–1902 | 20 | 7 | 2 | 13 | 16 | 7 | — | 1 |

not earned advanced degrees had done advanced work. By 1901–2 80 per cent of the teachers had earned an advanced degree and seven members of the faculty, or 35 per cent, had earned the Ph.D. degree. All but two of the faculty members of 1901–2 had done formal advanced work in their field of teaching. Five of the seven who held the Ph.D. degree had studied in American universities; the remaining two earned the degree in Germany. None of the seven was an Oberlin graduate. The College more and more looked to other institutions to supply candidates for its highest teaching positions. Recent graduates of Oberlin were often appointed to instructorships but they rarely remained more than a few years. After 1890 few teachers were shifted from one subject to another, a practice that had been very common in the old college. An exception was Lyman B. Hall who transferred from the professorship of Latin to that of history, but only after he had prepared himself by study in the graduate schools of three American universities. Oberlin had assumed the obligation of placing only professionally qualified teachers in its classrooms.

College officials tried to find teachers who combined competence in their work with loyalty to Oberlin's religious tradition. Although some new criteria for judging teachers had been adopted, the old were not discarded. In 1896 the board of trustees strongly reaffirmed the Christian character of Oberlin in an official statement on the recruitment of faculty. Oberlin teachers should be "persons of high scholastic attainment and of positive Christian character, capable of inspiring Christian principle and of developing Christian character in their students, persons in touch with the life of the world, and urgent to apply the Christian as distinguished from the materialistic philosophy to the living problems of this generation."[47] Teachers were expected to participate in the religious services. In 1898 a professor from the theological seminary was sent by the Committee on Appointments to inquire into the "religious position and influence" of a prospective college faculty member. He was authorized, if satisfied on these points, to offer the position.[48] The promotion of another teacher, a professor of English, to a permanent position was carefully reviewed because of his alleged indifference to family prayers, his lack of sympathy with missionary work, and his criticism of some church people for their opposition to the theater.[49] The personal habits of prospective faculty members were scrutinized for their conformity to Oberlin's idea of piety. Thomas N. Carver, when being considered in 1894 for appointment as associate professor of economics, was told by President Ballantine that "none of us here uses either liquor or tobacco. If either of these is necessary for your comfort, you will probably not care to consider this position." Happily, Carver was able to reply that he had been reared on principles of "strict teetotalism" in respect to both.[50] Ironically, an Oberlin graduate whom the College was eager to hire, Guy S. Callender, an economist at Yale University, declined to be considered for a position in part because of Oberlin's disapproval of smoking.[51]

Although the College cast its net somewhat farther, the task of finding, hiring, and retaining suitable faculty members was difficult. Many colleges and universities competed for the small number of professionally trained teachers. Even some Oberlin graduates could not be persuaded to accept positions on the faculty. Professional loyalties and opportunities for research were stronger pressures in some instances than devotion to alma mater. In 1896 Robert A. Millikan, who had graduated from Oberlin only five years before, was offered the professorship of physics which he declined in order to go to the University of Chicago as assistant to Professor A. A. Michelson. As Millikan recalled, the salary offered by Oberlin was twice the amount he was to receive at Chicago, but he was eager to share the "freedom and . . . the stimulating research atmosphere" of the university.[52]

The new conditions and opportunities in the teaching profession, which Millikan's decision illustrates, might alone have been sufficient to produce instability in the Oberlin faculty. Whatever the causes, a rash of faculty resignations deprived Oberlin of some of its ablest teachers. In the opinion of one professor, the faculty was never stronger in teaching ability than at the opening of Ballantine's presidency. However, five of the best teachers—William B. Chamberlain, William I. Thomas, Charles Harris, Harry H. Powers, and William G. Frost—resigned within a few years.[53] In most of these resignations financial problems and disappointments played some part. Oberlin salaries were low in comparison with those paid in comparable colleges, and many of the professors were "seriously overworked," as President Barrows confessed in 1898.[54] Some teachers, such as John R.

Commons, who spent one year at Oberlin as associate professor of political economy, would have preferred to remain but could not afford to decline a new position offering a substantially higher salary.[55] In other resignations money was indirectly involved. Charles Harris, the highly regarded professor of German, decided to leave because the College could not afford the books he needed for teaching and research.[56] Others, such as William I. Thomas and Harry H. Powers, became interested in new fields of learning and left for graduate training elsewhere.

Despite its many financial and personnel problems, Oberlin built upon the foundations of academic renewal laid in the previous decade. In many ways the opportunities for serious study were expanded. One important innovation was to bring the admissions and course requirements of the Philosophical and Scientific Courses, which had been set up for students who could not qualify for the bachelor of arts degree, into conformity with the higher standards of the Classical Course. After 1891 four years of secondary school preparation were required for admission to all the courses; completely uniform admissions standards were adopted in 1901 when the requirement of Greek for admission to the Classical Course was abolished.[57] Admissions requirements were then thoroughly revised, permitting students far more flexibility in the presentation of subjects for entrance.[58] By 1901 the differences between the courses had been entirely eliminated.[59] Henceforth, all Oberlin students took the same course and were awarded the same degree.

The elective principle continued to encroach upon the prescribed curriculum. The college catalogue assumed a modern appearance with listings of the many courses offered in each department. A large number of two- and three-hour electives were added in order that students could study more intensively subjects that especially interested them.[60] Most of the new courses were in philosophy, history, political economy, art, literature, mathematics, and the sciences. This expansion, according to President Ballantine, had not been lightly undertaken nor had it "gone in advance of needs, in theoretic lines; it has been forced upon us by the pressure of actual demands from students upon the ground." Ballantine claimed that Oberlin still lost some of its abler students because it did not offer sufficient advanced electives.[61] By 1901 course requirements had been further reduced.

Mathematics, English composition, and a course on the New Testament were the only required freshmen courses. For upperclassmen, courses in English, chemistry or physics, psychology, ethics or introductory philosophy, theology, and the Bible were required, but the remainder of the students' work could be chosen from the large number of electives.[62] The fixed curriculum of the liberal arts had almost vanished.

With fewer course requirements and many new courses offered, students could specialize to a much greater degree than ever before. Specialization permitted the use of methods of teaching that encouraged original work. Seminars were established in many departments. Essay contests, with cash prizes, were conducted by Professor James Monroe for his classes on political economy and modern history. In the past such artificial stimulants to scholarship had been scorned at Oberlin.[63] One faculty member proposed that a fund be established for the publication of the best papers of his history seminar.[64] Extracurricular study clubs began to appear. A scientific club for students interested in geology and zoology, and Greek, French, and German clubs were all founded in the early nineties.[65] Even the enlarged curriculum failed to satisfy the appetite of some students for knowledge. As President Ballantine said, an "increasing love for study," was manifesting itself in many ways among both students and faculty.[66]

Few, if any, subjects could rival the social sciences in student popularity and regard during the nineties. The extracurricular interest of Oberlin students in a wide range of current public questions carried over to affect the curriculum. Instruction in this field became more thorough and analytical as expert, university-trained young men were added to the faculty. The advent of professionalism also strengthened the cause of social reform. The Oberlin social scientists, like many of their colleagues elsewhere, believed that the ultimate purpose of studying society was its improvement. They were not detached clinicians, indifferently examining the workings of an intricate organism. Knowledge, they believed, should directly serve the reforming impulse.

In 1891 Professor James Monroe reached the age of seventy. Although sufficiently vigorous to teach for five more years, his age and the demand of students for advanced courses in the social sciences made it necessary to add another teacher. Monroe proposed that his former student, John R. Commons, be offered the position. While in college Commons had decided to study political economy after his graduation. Urged by Monroe and a fellow Oberlin student, Toyokichi Iyenaga, and drawn by the rising reputation of Professor Richard T. Ely, he enrolled at Johns Hopkins University in 1888.[67] Monroe wrote a laudatory letter of recommendation and persuaded two of Oberlin's trustees to lend Commons a sum sufficient to finance graduate studies.[68]

Commons left Johns Hopkins without obtaining his doctorate, but his experiences at the university were rewarding.[69] When he entered graduate school he was determined, so he later said, to begin with a clean mental slate in order to re-think his social principles.[70] When he returned to Oberlin his work was inspired by the new aims, concepts, and methods of political economy that were being formulated at Johns Hopkins. Professor Ely was the leader of a new school of historical political economists who discarded traditional economic theory resting on rigid, deduced laws of economic behavior, in favor of empirical generalizations derived from a "historical" study of the growth of economic institutions and changing economic, social, and political conditions. These historical political economists opened the way for a liberalization of economic thinking.[71] Commons was closely associated with Ely in research, class work, and many other scholarly tasks.[72] Both were convinced that the study of economics and society should lead directly to the solution of social problems. As Commons declared of political economy at this time, "there is no study that is not of help to [it]. It can utilize all the other sciences and combine them all to meet the one end for which they are valuable, the good of mankind."[73] Political economists should study and illuminate economic and social conditions and the leading issues in public policy, while as teachers they should lead students to an awareness of alternatives and encourage them to choose among different policies according to the highest moral values.

In May, 1891, Monroe recommended and the faculty approved a division of the courses in political economy and history between himself and Commons, who was then teaching at Wesleyan University in Connecticut. Commons was offered an associate professorship at $1200, with ten hours of teaching a week.[74] Because he was eager to write, this seemed a heavy load; however, he accepted the offer.[75] When he came to Oberlin Commons made an important change in his method of teaching. Instead of posing as an authority, he decided to share his curiosity, hopes, and doubts with his students.

> I determined . . . that I would spring on my students all of my inconsistencies, all of my doubts of economic theory, all of my little schemes of curing economic, political, and sociological disease. Perhaps that would interest them. And it did. . . . They could see that I was not an authority, did not know much of anything, but was getting ideas from them and incorporating their ideas into mine. I did not quit lecturing, or class quizzing. But my subject-matter was prosperity and depression; unions and unemployment; schemes that I was working on at the time; what the business men, farmers, laborers, politicians, were doing about it; what the economists' theories would lead them to; what I would do and you would do; and how we would justify it, if we could. Every class meeting or lecture was something unexpected, and they didn't know what was coming next. I was continually changing my mind. . . . It worked.[76]

To Ely, he wrote: "My position here is very pleasing to me. My classes are enthusiastic, and they take hold earnestly." [77] His first-term courses consisted of political economy for seniors, American institutional history, and sociology. These were the first college courses in American history and sociology to be offered at Oberlin. The text for the political economy course was E. Benjamin Andrews' *Institutes of Economics,* a work within the classical tradition although it departed in some respects from strict laissez-faire principles and emphasized current economic problems. Commons also assigned two of Ely's books, *Problems of Today* and *An Introduction to Political Economy,* in both of which current economic and social ills were carefully examined. Owing to the inadequacy of Oberlin's library, one dollar was collected from each member of the class to buy books for collateral reading.[78]

Although Commons taught only one year at Oberlin, he planned a thorough, new curriculum in economics, political science, sociology, and history that was largely implemented by his successors. The introductory course on political economy, which had been an elective for seniors, was made a required course for sophomores in order that students might have an opportunity to elect the advanced courses which were added. In this course Ely's textbook, *An Introduction to*

*Political Economy,* and "monographs on special topics" were used. Commons described the course as "mainly historical and descriptive, showing the development of modern industrial conditions and the significance of modern problems." [79] He proposed to add a large number of advanced electives in sociology including a course on social problems in which "Charities, Pauperism, Intemperance, Penology, Education, Immigration, Race Problems, the Family, and plans for social reform" [80] were studied. In economics, he proposed to offer a list of electives on institutional and historical subjects and, finally, he intended to continue offering courses in American and British history.[81] In addition to his work with undergraduates, Commons offered two courses of lectures in the short-lived extension program. One of these, called Political Economy and the Labor Problem, consisted of six lectures on such topics as wages and interest, rent and profits, poverty and pauperism, and plans for social reform, which covered everything from factory legislation to the single tax.[82] He tried to convey his reforming ardor combined with scholarship to the people of the surrounding countryside as well as to the students.

Commons' teaching and the planning of this new curriculum did not exhaust his abundant energy. He found time to support the cause of social reform in other ways. In November, 1891, he delivered an address before the Congregational Club of Cleveland on "The Christian Minister and Sociology." This address, published and distributed as a pamphlet by the Christian Social Union, was an impassioned plea to Christian ministers to uncover, define, publicize, and resolve social problems.[83] They had been, he charged, guilty of moral blindness and insensitivity in failing to protest against the development of rigid social classes. Although the ethical values of Christianity provided the proper standard by which to judge men and society, Christians acquiesced in social injustice because ministers had failed to provide leadership. They had confined themselves to the message of individual redemption, righteousness, and salvation, but these teachings, however important, failed to meet the pressing social needs of the times. Bad social conditions were the result of human will, ignorance, and indifference, not of natural laws, so by means of individual effort and positive legislation society could be transformed, controlled, and made righteous. Specifically, Commons urged ministers to work toward the establishment of institutional churches, to encourage their congregations to take a sympathetic interest in the poor, and to carefully instruct their congregations in the complexities of social problems. He thought that a minister might properly spend half of his time in the pulpit discussing the "fundamental relations and principles of society." Merely to preach brotherhood was insufficient. "People need not only the heart of love, but also the knowledge wisely to guide their love. . . . No off-hand philanthropy can excuse itself with the plea that the heart is right, therefore God will care for the results. Such a philosophy makes simply fanatics." [84] An urgent, unequivocal call for a social gospel had been sounded in Oberlin. Commons' essay aroused great interest there. The faculty, persuaded by his declaration that ministers should be experts in social relations, voted to give academic credit to seminary students who took either Commons' course in sociology or a new course of President Ballantine's on Christian Ethics, which was possibly intended as a moderating influence. [85]

During his year at Oberlin Commons was busy with many other projects. He compiled and published a *Popular Bibliography of Sociology* and worked on several lectures and articles which were later published. [86] He spoke to faculty meetings, delivered Thursday lectures to the students, and wrote critical reviews of debates and orations for the student newspaper. [87] In the spring of 1892 he resigned in order to accept a position at Indiana University. He left Oberlin regretfully because "there are strong personal ties binding me here, and the religious life is attractive to me," but the "University holds a higher place in scholarship," and it offered a larger salary. [88] In his year at Oberlin Commons introduced the modern teaching of the social sciences, and, by precept and example, in the classroom and out, he led Oberlin toward an abiding commitment to social Christianity.

Commons' two immediate successors, J. William Black (1892–94) and Thomas N. Carver (1894–1900), built upon the foundations he had laid. Black was a fellow graduate student of Commons' at Johns Hopkins University, where he received both his B.A. and Ph.D. He taught at Georgetown College, Georgetown, Kentucky, for a year before being appointed associate professor of political economy at Oberlin. [89] Most of Black's training was in history. His doctoral dissertation, written under the supervision of Professor Herbert Baxter Adams, was a study of Maryland during the French and Indian

War.[90] The Johns Hopkins graduate program, however, prescribed training in all of the social sciences, so Black was prepared to teach them all at Oberlin.[91] He continued the work that Commons had initiated with only minor changes, dropping some of the courses in economics and adding several in American and English history.[92]

Like Commons, Black believed that the purpose of studying society systematically was to enable one to work for its improvement. In a Thursday lecture he quoted with approval a remark of the anthropologist Edward B. Tylor, who had said that "the unconscious evolution of society is giving place to its conscious development, and the reformer's path of the future must be laid out on deliberate calculation from the track of the past."[93] Society suffered from anachronistic customs and institutions of primitive ages that should be excised.

Black's course on practical sociology, which was very popular with students and to which he devoted much time and effort, served as a guide to social reform. As one student recorded his remarks, the "practical side of Sociology implies discussion of [the] attitude of a free republican government to social question[s] and includes [the] duties of educated intelligent young men to social matters."[94] The object of social science "we consider . . . to be the Amelioration of Mankind."[95] In this course Black took up such topics as the causes of pauperism, the problems of the unemployed, the history of poor relief, and the work and effectiveness of private and public charitable organizations. The bibliography included works by such social critics and reformers as Henry George, Richard T. Ely, Charles Loring Brace, Charles Kingsley, Washington Gladden, Carroll D. Wright, and William J. Tucker. The textbook was Charles R. Henderson's *An Introduction to the Study of the Dependent, Defective and Delinquent Classes*.[96] Students wrote papers on "The Institutional Church," "The Problem of Child Labor," "The Life and Work of Arnold Toynbee," "Charles Kingsley," "The Work of Hull House," "The Tramp Problem and Legislation," and "The Drink Problem, Sociologically Considered."[97]

The Department of Political Economy thrived while Black taught at Oberlin. He told Professor Adams at Johns Hopkins in March, 1893, that the Department "is booming, and is larger than ever before."[98] One popular innovation of Black's, which he described as learning "à la Hopkins methods," was to arrange tours for students in order to illustrate from daily life the theories and materials that were studied in the classroom. In February, 1893, he took his advanced class in Economic Problems to Cleveland to observe industrial methods and factory working conditions. The purpose of the trip was to show "the extent to which the introduction of machinery has done away with skilled labor, and often reduced greatly the amount of unskilled labor required." [99] This class also helped to compile a bibliography called *References on the History of Labor and Some Contemporary Labor Problems,* which was published by Black in March, 1893. [100] The following year he took twenty-five "sociology enthusiasts" from the course on practical sociology to Cleveland for a "pleasant and profitable" trip visiting and examining public and private philanthropic and service organizations. [101] They visited the office of the Bethel Associated Charities, City Hall, the poor house, the city hospital, the work house, and the jail. The *Oberlin Review* reported that "The day from beginning to end though tiresome was most instructive, and the class is unanimous in feeling grateful to Professor Black for the treat." [102]

A second innovation was to invite outside speakers to discuss subjects under consideration in class. In March, 1893, Laurence Gronlund, the pioneer American socialist, spoke to the class in economic problems on "The Moral Regeneration of Our Country," arguing that socialism should replace an immoral competitive capitalism. [103] Robert Bandlow, a Cleveland labor leader, defended unions and their methods before the same class. The students "showed great interest in the subject and fired a volley of questions at the speaker." [104] Dr. L. B. Tuckerman of Cleveland lectured to the economics classes on "Materialism" and on "Money from a Populist's Standpoint." [105] Dr. Samuel Warren Dike, secretary of the National Divorce League, delivered four lectures on the family and divorce before Black's class in practical sociology, and he lectured to the seminary students on "Social Structure" and "The Relation of Sociology to the Ministry." [106]

Despite the popularity of the subjects with students, instruction in political science, economics, and sociology suffered during the lean years of the middle nineties when Oberlin passed through a financial crisis. The social sciences were relatively new to the curriculum, lacking the prestige of many older disciplines. The social science teachers, with the exception of James Monroe, were young men without the seniority others enjoyed. As Black remarked. "The hard times have struck us a severe blow." [107] Various expedients to reduce expenses were considered. The most desperate proposal called for the dismissal of the professor of political economy, the division of the introductory courses in that field among three of the older faculty members, and the abandonment of the advanced courses. Black was so depressed by the prospects that he sought a new position. In April, 1894, he resigned to become professor of history and political economy at Colby College.[108]

The faculty originally intended to leave Black's place unfilled. It soon became apparent, however, that this would be unsatisfactory. The students, especially the men, had come to expect and demand a full complement of courses in economics and sociology.[109] In the summer of 1894 Thomas N. Carver, a recent doctoral graduate of Cornell University, was appointed associate professor of economics. Carver had studied at Johns Hopkins University with Ely and John Bates Clark, as well as at Cornell.[110] At first he taught only economics. By 1895, however, it was clear that Oberlin could not immediately afford a sociologist as well as an economist, so he offered a full list of undergraduate courses in sociology.[111] Carver added two courses in economics to the curriculum. One was an advanced elective called The Distribution of Wealth, which he described as "a study of the modern distributive process, and the laws which determine the shares in the products of industry." Continuing the scrutiny of the morality of social relations begun by Commons and Black, the course included "a study . . . of the ethical basis of distribution and the features of the present system that are most often attacked as being contrary to ethical principles." [112] The course ended with an examination of contemporary society to determine "whether a radical change in social conditions is necessary." [113] A second new elective was Industrial Evolution, a historical study of the development of modern industrial processes and an analysis of their effect on the accumulation and distribution of wealth. In this course Carver made use of J. A. Hobson's recently published book on *The Evolution of Modern Capitalism*.[114] In 1895 Carver added an advanced economics course called Economic Legislation in which he had the students "draw up bills for legislative enactment and debate them in class. The purpose is to give the student some experimental knowledge of the difficulties in the way of reform by means of legislation, together with some theoretical knowledge of the principles of state interference"[115] In the field of sociology Carver continued to teach the popular course on practical sociology and he added courses on the state, anthropology, theory of social progress, and socialism.[116]

When Professor James Monroe retired in 1896 another burden was placed on Carver's shoulders. The financial strain precluded the appointment of a replacement so Carver was asked to offer four of Monroe's courses.[117] In three years the catalogue listed twenty-one different courses in economics, sociology, political science, and international law taught by Carver.[118] Hard times forced many teachers to attempt far more than they could effectively perform.

Carver has had a deserved reputation as an orthodox economist.[119] He brought a note of caution to the enthusiasm for reform that Black and Commons had helped to inspire. His distrust of the capacity of the state for constructive work and of man for disinterested action prevented him from promoting crusades. In a public lecture, entitled "The Social Problem," he took the position that the improvement of man and society would be difficult and slow in coming. The evolving, ameliorating force of religion might eventually produce better conditions, but the state could do little to promote or hinder the attainment of perfection.[120] As an economist Carver was chiefly interested while at Oberlin in the subject of the distribution of wealth. He believed that distribution in the United States did not accurately reflect the contribution of each class and individual to the production of wealth, nor did it conduce to a healthy society, but he was at a loss to know what could be done. Acknowledging ills in the existing order, he thought that most of the proposed remedies for social problems would produce worse evils than those they were supposed to eradicate.[121]

Carver was one of Oberlin's most popular teachers. By 1900 more hours were elected in economics by undergraduate men than in any other subject.[122] One student wrote in 1898: "Possibly Professor Carver is more closely connected with the upper-class men of the institution than any other of Oberlin's instructors, and the esteem in which he is held as a teacher is equalled only by the consideration shown him by noted economists as a strong and honest thinker."[123] By the time Carver resigned in 1900 in order to accept a position at Harvard, economics and sociology were firmly established in the Oberlin curriculum.

The need for reform that was publicized inside the classroom was reinforced without by speakers who appeared on campus under college auspices. Pre-eminent among them was Rev. Washington Gladden, who became closely associated with Oberlin after he was made pastor of the First Congregational Church in Columbus, Ohio, in 1882. He had already published several essays and books advocating social Christianity. His first speaking engagement at Oberlin was in May, 1883, when he delivered a Thursday lecture on "Poverty, Ignorance and Sin, Their Comparative Causes and Comparative Cures." [124] On numerous later occasions he spoke to college audiences on religious and reform subjects or exchanged pulpits with Oberlin pastors. His sermons and lectures were always highly praised. [125] In 1896, when he was elected to the Oberlin board of trustees, the *Oberlin Review* called him "one of Ohio's brightest thinkers" and predicted that he would be "a tower of strength among the trustees." However, he declined to serve, probably because of other commitments. [126] Gladden continued to be a very popular speaker at Oberlin after the turn of the century. His moderate yet far from negligible version of the social gospel closely accorded with the idea of reform embraced by most Oberlin students. Professor Richard T. Ely, Lyman Abbott, President John Bascom of the University of Wisconsin, Dr. J. W. Stuckenberg, and Jane Addams were a few of the many who spoke at Oberlin in the late nineteenth century on various topics from a social gospel standpoint. The warm reception they all received is another indication of Oberlin's sympathy with the movement. [127]

President William G. Ballantine, in his baccalaureate sermon of 1894, attempted the first official accommodation with social Christianity. Entitled "The Coming Day," the sermon was critical of selfishness and waste among both the very rich and the very poor. In lurid words the president portrayed national social conditions.

> Poverty, vice and wretchedness abound. Our annual drink bill is at the lowest estimate seven hundred millions of dollars. Corruption in politics, wasteful extravagance in private life, speculation and rapacity in business, morose unreasonableness among laborers, everywhere selfishness and self-indulgence, haste to get something for nothing and enjoy it grossly—the sight of these makes our hearts ache. [128]

Things could be set right by an enlightened paternalism modeled on the humble, serving life of Jesus, in which the educated would lead the masses toward a good society, averting the opposing catastrophes of disorder and injustice. Ballantine urged the new alumni to consider joining a settlement house, a charitable organization, or an institutional church, since each provided an effective way of moving toward the new day of Christian brotherhood.

Soon after this indication of the president's qualified sympathy with new forms and expressions of the ideal of service, more manifestations of Oberlin's interest in social Christianity appeared. In the fall of 1894 and the summer of 1895 conferences on Christian Sociology met there. While these conferences were not formally under the control of the College, they were planned and conducted by some of its officials, teachers, and friends. Z. Swift Holbrook, a Chicago businessman and academic adventurer whose star shone briefly at Oberlin, figured in the preparations for the conferences. His position on social issues was clear. In addresses and pamphlets he deplored the sentimentalism, the "altruistic tendency," which he asserted marked the thinking of most academic and religious students of society. They showed, he charged, an undue tenderness for the poor and the workingman. As a practical, hardheaded business man, he undertook to set others straight. Professor George F. Wright of the theological seminary, whose views were similar to Holbrook's, invited him to Oberlin to lecture.[129] In March, 1893, speaking on "The Lessons of the Homestead Troubles," he praised Henry Clay Frick, president of the Carnegie Steel Company, who broke the great Homestead strike, and castigated the assorted union leaders, demagogues, journalists, and clergymen who, he claimed, had misled the steel workers into a false view of their rights and interests.[130] One faculty member thought the lecture was "not altogether fair . . . [but it was] the first good showing we have had in opposition to the claims of labor." [131] While he expressed alarm at the great growth and the irresponsibility of industrial combinations, he was violently abusive of certain other organizations, doctrines, and persons: trade unions, socialism, anarchism, and the sentimentalists among sociologists and ministers. In his judgment, they all were threats to the foundations of the republic.[132] Workingmen should count their blessings, not covet the hard-won riches of others. Holbrook relied upon stern warnings against attacks on property and a vague appeal to Christian duty to preserve society. If the agitations provoked by ministers, academic sociologists, and ambitious union leaders were replaced with a patient concern for justice and respect for private rights, the republic would resume its triumphant march. These and similar ideas were expressed in a course of lectures on Christian sociology which Holbrook delivered to students during the winter term of 1895.[133]

The Institute of Christian Sociology, which Holbrook organized, met at Oberlin in November, 1894. A number of leading social gospel clergymen took part in its deliberations including Josiah Strong, Graham Taylor, and J. H. W. Stuckenberg. Washington Gladden, the "Nestor of Christian Sociologists," as the *Oberlin Review* called him, was elected president of the Institute. Oberlin itself was represented by Lucien Warner of the board of trustees, President Ballantine, Rev. Henry Tenney, the pastor of the Second Church, and Professor William I. Thomas, who was studying sociology at the University of Chicago while on leave from his teaching duties at Oberlin.[134] The Institute was to have been the first of a series of such conferences, and it was hinted that a Graduate School of Sociology and Economics might be established at Oberlin in which Holbrook doubtless would have played a prominent part had it ever materialized. The *Oberlin Review* urged "every student interested in the foremost topic of this age" to attend the Institute and suggested that the junior and senior classes be dismissed while it was in session.[135] Over two hundred persons from outside Oberlin attended the meetings.[136]

The major addresses were delivered by Stuckenberg, Gladden, Strong, Tenney, Warner, Thomas, and Holbrook. Stuckenberg, Gladden, and Strong showed a receptivity to effective measures for alleviating the conditions of life for the working classes and for restricting the irresponsible power of great wealth. The sharpest clash occurred between Thomas and Holbrook who differed radically and significantly in their conceptions of sociology. Holbrook claimed that the work of scientific sociologists was too speculative and abstruse to be useful in solving practical human problems. He favored a sociology based upon personal observation and subjective reasoning; in effect, a sociology that would contain whatever one wished to uphold. Thomas argued that a science of society was possible and he challenged the assertion that all social problems would promptly disappear if the spirit of Jesus Christ, however that might be defined, reigned in the world. Careful, objective observation and strict scientific reasoning, he believed, were necessary preliminaries to the accomplishment of lasting and just social reconstruction. The scientific sociologist, he implied, could furnish the only sure guidance in the tasks of reform. Any body of doctrine with less secure foundations would be only a receptacle for personal or class interest.[137]

A major task of the Institute was to prepare for the Summer School of Christian Sociology to be held in 1895. A committee of eight, with Gladden as chairman, was appointed to devise plans for the school. The general topic was "The Causes and Proposed Remedies for Poverty." The speakers, representatives of both capital and labor, were to deal with immediate problems as much as possible. Two academic thinkers participated: John Bates Clark, the Amherst College economist, and Stephen F. Weston, a sociologist of Western Reserve University. Gladden and Rev. Levi Gilbert of Cleveland represented the clergy. Businessmen were represented by S. P. Bush, a railroad executive, and N. O. Nelson of St. Louis, whose firm had pioneered in profit sharing. Among others present who were actively engaged in the search for solutions to current economic and social problems were Clarence Darrow; Jane Addams; Robert Bandlow, a Cleveland labor leader and journalist; James Sovereign, head of the Knights of Labor; Thomas Morgan, a Socialist writer; Carroll D. Wright, United States Commissioner of Labor, and Samuel Gompers, president of the American Federation of Labor. Oberlin talent included Holbrook, Thomas N. Carver, James Monroe, Edward I. Bosworth, and the two Congregationalist ministers, Henry M. Tenney and James Brand.[138]

The views expressed were as varied as the list of speakers would lead one to expect. Clark and Carver defended free competition as the only means of social improvement. Darrow and Holbrook debated the series of issues raised by the railroad strike of 1894. Holbrook presented a second paper on poverty in which he characteristically laid "more stress than many do on the faults of the individual."[139] In other addresses, Gompers defended the use of strikes. Carroll Wright argued that social and industrial conditions were slowly improving, Morgan appealed for a socialistic experiment, Jane Addams described the work at Hull House, and Gladden pointed out dangers to the nation arising from corporate wealth and an irresponsible use of power.[140] According to the *Oberlin Review*, "throughout the sessions the best of feeling existed among the representatives of the different classes although many of the discussions were very warm." [141]

The Summer School, it was hoped, would become an annual affair, but the necessary financial support could not be obtained.[142] The Institute and the Summer School did provide forums for the presentation of diverse views on the leading social questions of the day. They marked another step in Oberlin's alignment with social Christianity.

Among active reform movements of the nineties, none was more vigorously supported than prohibitionism. Although the situation of Oberlin itself was settled in 1882 with the passage of the Metcalf bill by the Ohio legislature, the Oberlin prohibitionists still had to be concerned about the evils of alcohol in the state and nation. In co-operation with other Ohio prohibitionist organizations, the Oberlin Temperance Alliance supported a series of local option bills. One of these, the Beatty bill, providing for a local option vote in townships, came up in the legislature in 1887. The Alliance decided to launch a campaign in its support under the leadership of Howard Hyde Russell, a student in the Oberlin theological seminary.[143]

Russell, later the founder and guiding spirit of the Ohio Anti-Saloon League, acquired valuable experience in the fight for the Beatty bill. Although he was thirty-one in 1887, he was only in his senior year in the seminary. As a young man he had been a Jack-of-all-trades. Following a dramatic sudden conversion, he had abandoned the law, his current profession, in order to prepare for the ministry.[144] The Temperance Alliance engaged Russell to work full time for the Beatty bill. Although he faced final examinations in the seminary, they were not allowed to hinder the more important objective. It was understood that the seminary faculty, because of its interest in prohibition, would be lenient with any shortcomings in his examinations. The faculty also agreed to supply Russell's student pulpit at nearby Berea, Ohio. He travelled throughout the state arousing temperance sentiment, bombarding the General Assembly with petitions and letters, and following this up with personal work in the lobby.[145] Until the last moment the passage of the bill was in doubt. Senator Crook of Dayton, who had pledged his vote in favor of the bill, informed Russell that pressures from his constituency forced him to reconsider. Russell hurried to Dayton, instituted a campaign of letters, telegrams, and personal interviews, and brought the senator back into line. Russell's efforts at this crucial moment were credited with securing the passage of the bill by the margin of a single vote.[146]

The subsequent history of legal prohibition in Ohio was bound up with Howard H. Russell and Oberlin. After the passage of the Beatty bill Russell hoped to organize a campaign for the extension of local option to the counties, but he presently left Ohio for Kansas City and later Chicago, where he met with unusual success in founding mission churches. He was still, however, convinced that his life's work lay in the prohibition crusade and so he maintained his association with Oberlin. Twice he spoke there urging the formation of a state prohibition organization. In 1893, when the Ohio State Liquor League was formed to uphold the interests of the liquor traffic, Russell proposed once again that he be appointed the agent of the Alliance to organize the state. His principal Oberlin correspondents were Giles W. Shurtleff, a college Latin teacher for many years but by 1893 its secretary and treasurer, and Frank F. Jewett, professor of chemistry and president of the Oberlin Temperance Alliance. Russell proposed to organize a state-wide, non-partisan temperance movement around the core of the Alliance. On May 24, 1893, at a meeting with Russell in the Spear Library on the college campus, the Alliance executive committee resolved to support a new organization to "unite the churches and all temperance people in an effort to awaken an interest and secure wise action in destroying the open saloon and securing individual total abstinence," and it pledged $500 toward Russell's salary as agent of the new organization.[147]

The Alliance membership ratified these decisions at a mass meeting on June 4, 1893, in First Church. Resolutions called for the formation of a "permanent and aggressive" organization, "in which all classes of the friends of temperance can unite," to be led by a full-time superintendent.[148] He was charged with developing and unifying temperance sentiment, securing enforcement of existing liquor legislation and working in behalf of the "enactment of further legislation in order that our people may be saved from the evils of the drink habit, and delivered from the debauching curse of the drink traffic."[149] One of the principal strengths of the new organization was its political impartiality. The division of prohibitionist forces between the Prohibition party and members of the major political parties had been a severe limitation on their effectiveness. The non-partisan character of the new movement was demonstrated by Professor A. S. Root, president of the Oberlin Prohibition Club, the local branch of the Prohibition party, who sat on the platform during the meeting and "pledged the support of the prohibitionists to the movement." [150] As the *Oberlin News* commented: "If other localities . . . will take hold with the zeal which has been shown here there would be an awakening throughout the state." [151]

Russell spent the summer of 1893 presenting the plan to audiences in northern Ohio towns and in preparing for a convention to complete the state organization. About $3,000 a year for three years was pledged.[152] Invitations to attend the convention, sent to churches and temperance organizations, met with a heartening response, and on September 5, 1893, the Ohio Anti-Saloon League was born at First Church.[153] A slate of officers was selected representing all parts of the state. Within a year three hundred local committees were in operation, a state paper, the *Anti-Saloon,* was being published, and $8,000 had been raised.[154] The Ohio Anti-Saloon League was one of the most successful state prohibition organizations. In addition to its influential role in Ohio life and politics, it fathered the Anti-Saloon League of America. Its techniques of leadership and mobilizing public opinion were copied by the national body when it came into existence.[155] Howard H. Russell served as state superintendent of the Ohio League until 1895 when he became general superintendent of the national League. He later organized the Lincoln-Lee Legion in Oberlin, the "moral suasion" arm of the League, which solicited abstinence pledges among young people.[156] Years later, after repeal of the Eighteenth Amendment, Russell came out of retirement to begin a new crusade for American and world prohibition.

Many Oberlin alumni played a part in the organized prohibition movement after 1893. None was better known or more effective than Wayne B. Wheeler, who led the Ohio Anti-Saloon League to a number of stunning political victories and, as general counsel of the Anti-Saloon League of America and its legislative representative during the twenties, presided over the amendment enforcement struggles of the drys. A diligent, pious student, Wheeler worked his way through the preparatory department and the College. As janitor in one of the college buildings he received fifteen cents an hour and the use of a room in its tower. For his meals he waited on tables and served as chaplain in a boarding house. From these labors, with vacation earnings, he met all of his college expenses and even had a small sum saved when he graduated.[157]

Wheeler became interested in the prohibition movement at Oberlin. He attended the meeting of June 4, 1893, at which the cause of the Anti-Saloon League was first presented to Oberlin citizens, and he pledged twenty-five cents a month to Russell's support. As he later wrote: "The simplicity and practical nature of the new organization captured me. It offered a chance for united effort to people who disagreed on nearly everything else. . . . It ignored all sectarian, political, racial, sectional or other subdivisions." [158] In 1894, Russell, in need of an assistant, inquired of various faculty members who recommended Wheeler for the position. At first he was not inclined to accept Russell's offer because the salary was so modest and he had decided on a career in business. After they prayed together, however, Russell overcame Wheeler's reluctance. He immediately plunged into his work, speaking in churches and organizing temperance sentiment in legislative districts, and soon became an expert in methods of legislative pressure and legal battling. To enhance his services he studied law at Western Reserve University, reading his law books in trains and hotel rooms as he went about the state on League business. He steadily rose through the ranks of the prohibitionist organization. As the "dry boss" of the twenties, he stood for the strictest enforcement of the national prohibition laws.

Although prohibition had ceased to be an important local issue, as a worthy state and national cause it continued to be supported by many alumni and teachers. Public meetings were occasionally held at Oberlin to debate proposed legislation and to take political stands, to support the work of the Anti-Saloon League, and to hear temperance speakers. Now and then an issue sparked a resurgence of activity. Such, for example, was the campaign of the Republican governor, Myron T. Herrick, for re-election in 1905, which posed a dilemma for Oberlinians. The town had been staunchly Republican since the fifties, but Governor Herrick was the spokesman of the Ohio wets. When he was renominated by the Republicans, Oberlin people had to choose between deserting the party of abolitionism and voting for a wet. The result was for many the first, and doubtless the last, desertion of the Republican ticket. One member of the faculty, polling his colleagues, found that forty-six refused to vote for Herrick, two probably would not vote for him, two would vote for him, and four were undecided.[159] Herrick campaigned in Oberlin on the day before the election, but the town gave its majority to the Democratic nominee and winner, John Pattison. The other Republican candidates received a large plurality in Oberlin as they did in the rest of the state.[160]

The excitement generated by the Herrick campaign was a rarity in prohibition history at Oberlin after the turn of the century. The Temperance Alliance infrequently met and the annual meeting of its executive committee became a formality. There were no local goals to which zeal could be directed, while state and national campaigns were now in the hands of professionals. In addition, scattered signs indicated that the more diverse Oberlin faculty of the early twentieth century was not unanimous in support of dry principles. The once frequent denunciatory "old-time Prohibition" speeches, which still occasionally could be heard, were not appreciated by everyone.[161] Two professors, a tiny minority to be sure, refused to vote for prohibition in a county local option canvass in 1908.[162] In 1915 some Oberlin teachers doubted the practicality and wisdom of a proposed state prohibition amendment on the grounds that it would not be approved by a majority sufficient to insure compliance. Possibly, too, a few members of the faculty actually favored a wet community.[163]

Among Oberlin students the temperance and prohibition causes continued to receive routine support. After the nineties, however, topics connected with prohibition rarely occupied a place in the programs of the literary societies.[164] Intemperance, it was argued, often went hand in hand with other wasteful and immoral practices of the poor, but more and more it was thought to be a symptom rather than the cause of personal and social ills. By the twentieth century few would have agreed with Fairchild's assertion that liquor was "the demon of the land." The prohibition movement had been relegated to a minor place in the hierarchy of reform.

In the nineties, when many institutions reached out in new directions, Oberlin adopted certain innovations. A few members of the faculty and alumni proposed that the College should try to become a university. This ambition led to various claims and projects, some representing only wishful thinking or an attempt to change the popular image of the College. References to Oberlin as a "university" in writings and speeches became common. President Ballantine suggested that the theological seminary had been doing work of university caliber all along, thus furnishing a strong foundation on which to erect a graduate school.[165] When former President Fairchild published an exposition of his theological beliefs in *Theology, Natural and Revealed*, Ballantine claimed the work indicated Oberlin's assumption of a university's responsibility "to send forth in books the mature results of research and reflection."[166] The establishment of a lecture series was cited to support Oberlin's claim to university standing.[167] In 1898, more significantly, the faculty and trustees instituted an earned Master of Arts degree program requiring a year of study and the satisfaction of departmental requirements.

One of the more ambitious but least successful of these projects was the attempt to launch an extension service. Offering lecture courses on a variety of subjects to anyone who wanted them and could pay a fee was a new university enterprise of the age. In 1891 Ballantine reported that university extension "has been taken up with enthusiasm by our Faculty."[168] A committee drew up a prospectus that included more than twenty courses in such different fields as Latin, philosophy, Church history, chemistry, mathematics, biology, geology, English literature, German, elocution, bibliography, and political economy.[169] The Oberlin professors hoped that classes would be organized in nearby towns by local university extension associations formed for that purpose and by existing organizations such as Y.M.C.A.'s, Chautauqua circles, and workingmen's associations. Although the lecturer's fee of ten dollars was reasonable, the extension system never took hold. No more than a handful of courses was given. An attempt to arouse interest in Cleveland failed, while the sparsely populated rural areas surrounding Oberlin did not offer a suitable field for the pursuit of learning on a part-time basis.[170] The failure of university extension signified the failure of the grandiose ambition to transform Oberlin into a university. Structural reorganization as a university and a formal change of title from college to university were rejected by the faculty and board in 1895–96.[171] Given Oberlin's location, traditions, and financial problems, the attempt to turn it into a modern university was bound to fail.

The philosophical foundations of Oberlin, subjected to some re-examination in the eighties, continued to receive consideration. Ballantine, Barrows, and other spokesmen stressed Oberlin's Christian commitment, but they agreed that students should be encouraged to pursue their studies in greater depth and with detachment. In 1896 the board of trustees, issuing a formal statement of aims, declared: "The original purpose of the founders of this institution is recognized and re-affirmed, namely—That this shall be a distinctively Christian institution, which aims to furnish the best attainable intellectual and moral training in all its Departments." [172] A new statement in the catalogue declared that Oberlin, an "avowedly Christian college" from its beginning, still intended

> to lay a practical, daily emphasis on the ethical and spiritual in education—on life and faith, and at the same time to allow the fullest freedom of thinking within the broadest Christian lines. The College . . . [believes] in a loyalty to Christian truth that should manifest itself in a persistent and earnest application of that truth to the life of the world.[173]

It was evident, however, as President Barrows added, that "the emphasis of the Christian life" had been somewhat changed, although "the forces which make for character and consecration to the Kingdom of Christ are as active and powerful as ever." [174] Former President Fairchild, still a close observer of Oberlin life, also conceded that there was "less distinct impulse to cultivate religious experience, and less intensity of experience than formerly," but, he thought, it would be "hasty" and "ill-judged" to say that the religious life of Oberlin had become superficial. The call of Christian duty was still answered when it came.[175]

The old evangelicalism was showing signs of wear. During the nineties the requirements for religious worship were significantly relaxed for the first time. In 1892 college men and women were permitted to substitute attendance at Y.M.C.A. meetings for the regular Sunday evening preaching service, a privilege which was extended to all Oberlin students four years later regardless of the branch of the institution in which they were enrolled.[176] In 1898 students were relieved of the obligation to attend any kind of second religious service on Sunday.[177] The rule stipulating morning prayers in student boarding houses was rescinded in 1901, although it was hoped that they would be continued voluntarily.[178] A suggestion popular with some students was the substitution of voluntary for compulsory attendance at daily chapel, but the faculty would not be pushed to that extreme.[179] Daily chapel and the class prayer meetings were increasingly defended, however, on a social rather than a religious basis. The services allegedly provided opportunities for forming friendships, afforded a "pleasing relaxation from the daily studies," and added "a wholesome influence to what makes up College life." [180] The Day of Prayer for Colleges continued to be an important occasion in Oberlin religious life. Still, the fact that Professor King began an article in support of observance of the Day of Prayer with the rhetorical question "Need the day be a bore to any thinking man?" surely indicated a fear that many students were unsympathetic.[181] The custom of opening classes with a prayer or hymn slowly died out. Since this was a matter of custom, not of rule, no formal change was made; it simply disappeared as the old faculty stepped down. As early as 1891 a student writer had questioned the value of maintaining a custom that had become an empty ritual for many faculty members and students.[182]

Revivals in the nineties were less frequent and finally they disappeared altogether. In the fall term of 1890 Rev. B. Fay Mills, a young revivalist with a mild social gospel message, held a two-week revival meeting under the sponsorship of the local churches and the College.[183] Classes were dismissed for two days to facilitate student attendance and participation. The refusal of the Conservatory of Music officials, who were associated with the College but not under the control of its faculty, to co-operate by dismissing their classes was greatly lamented by some of the college faculty.[184] Mills' sermons were clear, logical, and "noticeably free from rant or appeal to the emotions." The *Oberlin Review* believed these qualities would recommend them to college students.[185] One observer, claiming student conversions numbered in the hundreds, declared there had been no equal revival since the days of Finney.[186] Yet revivalism declined quickly after 1890. The last important one occurred early in 1895 when Rev. A. M. Hills conducted meetings. Again the accounts stressed the "entire absence of all gush and mere sentiment," but, regardless of the preacher's restraint, the college students were mostly indifferent.[187] The revival did not result in many conversions, although it was claimed it had contributed to a deepening of student spirituality. President Ballantine encouraged revivals and reported their results in optimistic terms, but Barrows made no effort of this kind.[188] The decline of revivalism did not, of course, mean that Oberlin had become indifferent to the fate of the student's soul. It signified rather that greater reliance would be placed upon Bible study and training classes as means of encouraging and guiding Christian living.[189] The students apparently believed that the new religious climate, calmer and less obtrusive, would prove to be a healthier and no less sincere expression of devotion and faith than the evangelicalism and demonstrative piety of the past.[190]

A somewhat freer student social life also began to emerge in the nineties. For many years there had been sporadic complaint about certain social rules. Many men, for example, were irritated by the requirement that they be in their rooms by ten o'clock in the evening.[191] In 1898, in the first significant liberalization, the ten o'clock rule was abolished. The self-reporting system, which apparently had been ignored for years, was abolished for juniors and seniors and two years later abolished for all students. Junior and senior women were allowed greater freedom on Sundays. All students were permitted to play cards.[192] The reasons for these changes given by Professor King, chairman of the faculty in the absence of a president, were that Oberlin students had become more aware of the freedom allowed their fellows in other colleges, that the trend of the times was to grant students greater responsibility for their behavior, and that it was incongruous for a college which preached the efficacy of moral and spiritual conviction to feel "the necessity of solving so many questions by pure requirement." [193] Other considerations, such as the decline in the proportion of men enrolled in the College and the pleasure a few of the faculty found in the indulgence of such minor vices as card games, may also have played a part.[194] Some faculty members and doubtless many alumni considered these steps an unwise and unnecessary compromise with the ways of the world.[195] Among the students, on the other hand, the changes in rules, limited as they were, were said to create a new spirit of harmony and loyalty.[196]

That the tone and content of Oberlin's academic, social, and religious commitments changed in the nineties was generally recognized. The influence of an urban student and alumni constituency, of the affiliated but autonomous Conservatory of Music with its less evangelical faculty and student body, of a more diverse college faculty, and of the insistent need for higher intellectual standards were all cited as important factors in undermining the old Oberlin system of piety and the academic and social practices that were a part of it.[197] Some alumni, students, and faculty believed no effort should be spared to insure that "the spirit of the former days [does] not disappear with the changes that are being made."[198] The characteristic religious and moral impetus of old Oberlin should not be sacrificed for higher academic standards. One alumnus wrote in 1895: "Really the old Oberlin is passing away. That is quite right, if only the old spirit of self-sacrifice can be maintained. It distresses me that the educational part in our colleges is not more thoroughly permeated with the Christian spirit, and education is looked upon so much as an end in itself."[199] Actually, there was little danger that Oberlinians would look upon learning as an end in itself. Even the most outspoken student and alumni critics of Oberlin's academic work failed to take that advanced position.

The old evangelicalism was attacked as an obstacle to the acquisition of knowledge and to the training of an inquiring, critical mind, but even the needed higher academic standard was conceived of as a way of attaining essentially religious ends.[200] One senior, F. N. Spindler, struck by the absence of a tradition of intellectual independence, argued that Oberlin evangelicalism was detrimental to the development of dedication to scholarship. Some students ignored their studies in the heat of religious enthusiasm, "forgetting that one serves God better by conscientious scholarly work than by neglect of study for artificial religious exertion."[201] Some faculty members, he claimed, yielded to the temptation to excuse lapses in scholarship in an especially devout student. Academic work would improve at Oberlin, he thought, only as religion became "more ethical and practical, and not so conventional and heated."[202] Spindler's attack upon the old evangelicalism continued after his graduation from Oberlin when, as a student at Harvard University, he wrote several letters to the *Oberlin Review* praising Harvard's recognition of intellectual and religious freedom.[203]

The relation between the objectives and needs of learning and the duty of religion was important for Oberlin. In the past, learning had been subordinated to the demands of evangelicalism. Some alumni, students, and teachers believed that Oberlin now needed principles that would preserve the ideals of religious, moral, and social service while allowing learning a less restricted development. E. Dana Durand, a young alumnus, assessing Oberlin from the perspective of recent experience in a leading university, charged that it had been hampered by an incorrect understanding of the ties between religion and learning.[204] Scholarship had been sacrificed in order to maintain a special religious environment. Cautiously he wrote of Oberlin:

> I sometimes question whether in her stress upon the right personal relation of the soul to God, she has not, by a mere shade, perhaps, neglected to emphasize sufficiently the duty of training the mind for service to the world—service which can be as real and as truly religious if it takes other forms than that of direct spiritual teaching.[205]

The essence of religion, he believed, lay in worthy service to God and mankind, so faith required every man to develop his power to serve to the greatest extent. Service through knowledge should be Oberlin's motto. If "this moral side of scholarship" was recognized, hard study would become the rule in college life.[206] In the future, good intentions, personal piety, religious conviction, and moral passion alone would not suffice to produce the best result. They had to be joined in a mind sharpened by exacting training, a proper instrument for the pursuit of knowledge.

## CHAPTER IV

# THE PROGRESSIVE ERA

Oberlin and the American people entered the new century with hope reborn. The stormy years of the nineties had been safely weathered. Oberlin emerged essentially unharmed from financial crisis, faculty change and dissatisfaction, and discontinuity in presidential leadership. The nation passed on from the challenges of financial heterodoxy, violent social conflict, and a war of aggressive imperialism. To be sure, neither the College nor the American people could claim that final answers had been given to all of the questions raised during the nineties. Yet, between the Spanish war and World War I, a bright optimism glowed at Oberlin and in the nation.

Progressivism defined the political mood of most middle-class Americans in the early twentieth century. The term had various meanings but for nearly all Americans its core consisted of making politics more democratic and maintaining open access to wealth and social status. This traditional formula, it was held, would lead to a bright future.

At Oberlin too there was a reassertion of tradition as the new century opened. Many college alumni and friends thought a serious risk had been taken in 1898 when John Henry Barrows was elected to the Oberlin presidency. An urbane non-Oberlinian, Barrows, they feared, would lead Oberlin far in the direction of liberal religion and eastern culture. With his early death in 1902, an unexpected opportunity occurred to redirect the College through a new president toward more familiar goals.

Henry Churchill King had served a long apprenticeship for the Oberlin presidency. Following his graduation from Oberlin and advanced studies at Harvard, he had held several teaching and administrative positions, thus acquiring familiarity with many of the College's activities. On two earlier occasions he had received sub-

stantial faculty and trustee support for election to the presidency. His
religious position was attuned to Oberlin's traditions and needs. A
religious liberal, he was, nevertheless, reassuringly evangelical in
tone and practice. He could effectively mediate between the evangelical past of Oberlin and contemporary religious liberalism.

King's election in 1902 was commonly viewed as a reaction against
the worldliness of the Barrows regime.[1] Three trustees strongly opposed his election in the belief that Oberlin needed more of the
broad-gauged, public-conscious leadership that Barrows had provided.[2]
King, with some other faculty members, had played an important part
in the recent, partial liberalization of student social and religious life,
but he was not identified with the more secular cultural and social
tone which Barrows represented. Minister, experienced teacher, student of Scripture, and theologian, he seemed to many alumni and
students to represent a return to the ways of the past.[3] From 1902
until 1917, when the war took King abroad first as a Y.M.C.A.
official and then as a diplomat, he represented, as well as one
person could, the aspirations and ideals of Oberlin. Signs of a
shift toward cultural pluralism can be discerned, but until 1917
King's efforts to hold fast to traditional principles were substantially
successful. World War I and its aftermath disclosed some of the
weaknesses in religiously consecrated education and genteel culture
at Oberlin as elsewhere. Prewar leaders, such as King, were never
comfortable in the postwar world.[4]

The composition and characteristics of the college board of trustees
in 1902 contrasted in several important ways with the board of 1866.
The alumni, with seventeen of the twenty-four members, had captured the board.[5] Only four trustees lacked a baccalaureate degree
either from Oberlin or elsewhere. The places of residence of board
members revealed a greater reliance upon urban areas for college
leadership. Only six trustees, all residents of Oberlin, lived in a small
town. The rest were scattered throughout the large cities of the north-
eastern quarter of the United States with concentrations in Cleveland, New York, and Chicago. The leading alumni of the College,
those who, it was thought, could best discharge the responsibility of
formulating principles and policies, were now to be found in the expanding cities where wealth and talent were gathered. A greater
proportion of the members of the board were in business and the

secular professions. Nine were businessmen, active in such different fields as banking, asphalt paving, and various kinds of manufacturing; and there were five lawyers, four teachers, and one doctor. The clerical group of five was proportionately only half as large as the same group in 1866. By 1917 the proportion of Oberlin graduates, city residents, and businessmen on the board had all slightly increased.

Oberlin alumni recovered some lost ground on the faculty during the King administration, giving substance to the claim of a return to older ways. Under Ballantine and Barrows the composition of the faculty had become more diverse than ever before. By 1901–2, only seven teachers, out of a total of twenty, had received all or a part of their education at Oberlin. President King sought to increase the representation of Oberlin graduates on the faculty and, at the same time, to appoint only teachers with the highest professional qualifications. Both aims were substantially accomplished. In 1917 the academic faculty, consisting of all those teaching academic subjects with the exception of instructors in physical education, numbered fifty-seven [6]—nearly a three-fold increase over 1902. Twenty-nine, or 51 per cent, held at least one Oberlin degree and eight, or 14 per cent, had received all of their higher education at Oberlin. These proportions are reduced by using the permanent faculty as the base figure—forty-seven—thus excluding all teachers of the rank of instructor, who rarely had graduate degrees and nearly all of whom were Oberlin alumni. On this basis, twenty-one faculty members, or 45 per cent, were Oberlin graduates but only one teacher on the permanent staff had been educated entirely at Oberlin.

Those of the permanent academic faculty in 1917 with an earned higher degree in their academic discipline numbered forty-two, or 89 per cent; the number with some formal advanced training, with or without degree, was forty-four, or 94 per cent; and the number with the Ph.D. degree was thirty-one, or 66 per cent. In 1901–2, 80 per cent of all teachers had earned an advanced degree, 90 per cent had undertaken at least some professional formal study beyond the bachelor's degree, but only 35 per cent had earned the Ph.D. degree. Only three members of the faculty in 1917 held a theological degree, two being graduates of the Oberlin theological seminary, and all three were close to retirement. Two of them had secured substantial formal advanced work in their fields of teaching. The most important changes then in the training of the faculty down to 1917 were the gradual increase in the proportion of Oberlin graduates (reflecting a greater degree of professional training for teaching among the alumni, as well as President King's policy), the steady increase in advanced training among the faculty as a whole, especially as evidenced in the remarkable increase in the number of those who had earned the Ph.D. degree, and the virtual disappearance of the teacher of liberal arts subjects trained in theology.

Oberlin authorities still inquired closely into the religious beliefs and personal habits of prospective faculty members. President King, writing to a Congregationalist official, said "There is no question at all that, other things being equal, . . . a man's Christian belief and enthusiasm do count in his election to the faculty." King listed four qualities which "a truly successful member of the faculty" must possess: adequate training, teaching power, "some breadth and depth of personality", and "a genuine Christian purpose." [7] The choice between two candidates for an instructorship in German turned in part upon their religious commitment. According to one of the more conservative members of the faculty, the first candidate was better prepared and probably a more effective teacher but a "Unitarian in church connection." The second candidate was "more promising in character —his western birth training and experience [sic] would fit him better for our work." He was, in addition, the son of a Methodist minister and had high character recommendations from an old Oberlinian. The faculty finally decided to appoint the former candidate, "provided he were willing to take up the religious responsibilities of the place," such as taking his turn at leading chapel service. As it turned out, he declined the offer.[8] Despite efforts to maintain an evangelical faculty, the exigencies of the situation required a measure of compromise. Several signs indicate that some of the young instructors and professors were uncomfortable under the constraints on their private lives and beliefs that Oberlin imposed, and unhappy with the emphasis, as they saw it, on moral and religious training at the expense of scholarly work.[9]

The bachelor of arts curriculum, the only course of study offered in these years, changed very little. Some changes in course requirements were made in 1911 such as the abandonment of one semester of required Senior Bible, the adoption of a scheme of concentration through a major system, and the addition of required subjects in the social sciences.[10] In 1913, after long faculty consideration and debate, limits were set on student participation in extracurricular activities in an attempt to ensure that a larger portion of the students' time would be given to study.[11] Standards of admission and the grade average required for graduation were raised while provision was made for graduation with honors in major subjects. As further evidence of an advance in academic standards, a Phi Beta Kappa chapter was established in 1907. Without dramatic change, academic work continued steadily to improve.[12]

Student ranking of educational objectives revealed the more prominent place occupied by scholarship. In 1911 the faculty Committee on Student Work and Life asked students to rank eleven possible goals of college work in their order of importance. The forms were returned by 62.5 per cent of the students, with a high proportion from the upper two classes. As the committee chairman noted, the respondents were probably the more earnest and sober of the students, so the results were "more ideal than the reality." [13] The order of importance among categories as ranked by all students is illustrated by the following list; separate listings of preferences by sex are shown in columns one and two.

|  | *Men* | *Women* |
|---|---|---|
| 1. Development of mental powers. | 1 | 2 |
| 2. Acquisition of general culture.. | 4 | 1 |
| 3. Development of moral character | 2 | 3 |
| 4. Acquisition of knowledge ..... | 3 | 4 |
| 5. Fitness for a particular vocation | 5 | 5 |
| 6. Social enjoyment and friendship | 7 | 7 |
| 7. Preparation for social service... | 8 | 6 |
| 8. Development of religious life.. | 6 | 8 |
| 9. High grades in studies....... | 9 | 9 |
| 10. Admission to Phi Beta Kappa.. | 11 | 10 |
| 11. Distinction in athletics....... | 10 | 11 |

Though the figures doubtless fail to reflect exactly the actual motives and convictions of all students, still they do indicate their serious purpose and show the displacement of religious by intellectual goals.

The general category of character development was high on the list, but the "development of religious life," implying the experience of conversion and steady growth in piety, ranked only eighth among the eleven choices.

More light was thrown on student values by a second questionnaire distributed by the same committee, which asked students to indicate how they spent their time. Students estimated that they spent forty-two hours each week on their studies and twenty-six hours divided among fourteen other activities.[14] The average number of hours per week spent in each activity by the student body as a whole and by those participating in selected activities is indicated below:

|  | All Students | Participants |
|---|---|---|
| Self support | 5.34 | 13.3 |
| Exercise | 4.01 | 5.0 |
| Social activities | 3.96 | 4.5 |
| Voluntary reading | 3.09 | 3.6 |
| Religious activities | 2.88 | 3.6 |
| Music | 2.02 | 5.6 |
| Amusements | 1.91 | 2.3 |
| Athletics | 1.08 | 4.0 |
| Literary society work | .83 | 3.0 |
| Boarding house organizations | .33 | 1.6 |
| Editorial work | .25 | 3.5 |
| Student Senate and Class work | .25 | 1.7 |
| Departmental Clubs | .15 | 1.3 |
| Other Organizations | .12 | 1.7 |

These student estimates indicate, most significantly, a moderate decline in participation in religious activities and a sharp drop in participation in the literary societies since the days of the evangelical college.

The reputedly unique spirit of Oberlin was a matter for pride among students. As one wrote in a freshman composition, "You do not find an aristrocracy ignoring the common, the rich treading on the rights of the poor, or the brilliant condemning the stupid."[15] Oberlin, "strangest of all," treated Negro students on an equal basis.

"Hardly could there be found another place in the union where a white man might walk arm in arm down the street with a negro and still retain his respectability."[16] Easy acceptance and social equality characterized relations between rich and poor students. Those who supported themselves were accepted on equal terms with those who spent their parents' money. Work was no disgrace; in fact, most student leaders in all kinds of activities were at least partially self-supporting. The instructor who graded the composition thought that this student's enumeration of the characteristics of Oberlin life was accurate but believed he unfairly denied many of the same qualities to other colleges.[17]

As Oberlin entered the twentieth century, the old evangelical faith, with its emphasis on individual salvation and personal moral codes, was giving way to a new faith combining reverence for the worth of the individual with social redemption. Respect for persons and social redemption were interdependent: each was necessary for the fulfillment of the other and both were necessary for the fulfillment of the divine plan for mankind. This transformation was manifested in word and deed: in the value attached to learning, in religious instruction and worship, and in social rules, as well as in the statements of students, faculty, and officials. As a formal doctrine, it was primarily the work of Henry Churchill King.

In many addresses and books as well as in the classroom he reinterpreted the social dimension of Oberlin's theological tradition. Among the general influences necessitating a reconstruction of theology King pointed to the "deepening sense of the value and sacredness of the person."[18] This included a new view of man and a new recognition of Jesus Christ "as the supreme person of history." King believed that "the greatest outcome of an advancing civilization is the deepening sense of the value of the individual person. This is the very flower and test of civilization."[19] That the individual was held in greater respect than ever before was for him beyond dispute. The sacredness of the person was both a description of an actual tendency in human relations and a fundamental ethical principle. From it derived "the unity of the ethical life in love."[20] It led to the recognition of the whole man and to a quickening of social conscience. It was incompatible with both a mechanistic view of human nature and a sacramentalism which found holiness in things rather than persons. The sacredness of the person included recognition of Jesus Christ as the supreme person in history. Modern methods of study and research, by adding to understanding of Jesus, had focused attention upon him with the result that faith in Christ as the supreme revelation of God was more profound and secure. The God with whom men came into personal relation was a God revealed concretely in the spiritual personality of Jesus. Greater knowledge had also resulted in a new understanding of Jesus' humanity. "Historical criticism has brought us into the very presence of the *man* Jesus, and has renewed for us, therefore, the gospel's own emphasis on the humanity of Christ, almost forgotten by the church in spite of both Gospels and creeds." [21] Thus could mankind feel a greater kinship with Jesus and, through him, with God.

The personal relationship was, for King, the key to the reconstruction of theology. The fundamental Christian religious relation was the filial relation to God through Christ. This "commonplace," if rejuvenated and given its rightful place at the center of theology, would ensure to Protestant Christianity, King believed, a vital role in the future. The ideal practice of religion for the individual was "to come into such ethical and spiritual relations to God as those in which Christ stood . . . [which were] first and foremost . . . *personal* relations." [22] Friendship among men and friendship between man and God were parallels. In each case mutual trust, common interests, and self-sacrifice were required. Friendship was the result of unconscious growth rather than of conscious arrangement. The experience could not be contrived but must be patiently awaited as the product of certain conditions. Constant association was the primary condition for deepening the divine friendship:

> We are to stay in the presence of Christ, to give him a chance at us, by attention, by thought, by taking his point of view and studying his thought, by getting into touch with his feeling and his purpose—living in his atmosphere. We can be sure of the effects in character and friendship.[23]

There had to be finally a "*sacred respect for the personality of the other.*" [24] Neither God nor man could make unjust demands. The recognition of friendship as the principal mode of Christian life and worship constituted, King thought, "the nearest approach man can make to the final realities of religion." [25]

King's reconstruction of theology in terms of personal relations brought together elements of traditional worship, respect for modern learning, and his interpretation of the contemporary ethos.[26] The need to cultivate the divine friendship justified anew many evangelical practices. Daily prayer, Bible study, and regular worship were necessary to its fulfillment. But piety could not be forced or artificially contrived. In order to contribute to the divine friendship, it must spring from the inner, voluntary reverence of the worshiper.

The theology of personal relations also implied social redemption. In *Theology and the Social Consciousness* King explained how a developing social consciousness affected theology. Social consciousness was the sense of the brotherhood of men. It was characterized by like-mindedness, reflecting both common influences and a confidence in the value and sacredness of each person. Social consciousness was required for the highest development of religious faith. Its influence on religious thinking had restored the social emphasis of Jesus to its rightful place in Christian belief. King believed that one could see in the world "the principle of personality fulfilling the will of God in social service."[27] The "application of the ethics of Christ to every social problem," as he had said earlier, would be the key task of the twentieth century.[28] God and man together would bring about social salvation. Through a theology of personal relationship King supplied Oberlin with a social Christianity.

The turn toward social redemption was graphically illustrated in the new, social purpose of organizations and practices which had earlier served as agencies of the old evangelicalism. After 1900, the YMCA and the YWCA, for example, emphasized social service.[29] They initiated a host of activities designed to aid in establishing the Kingdom of God on earth. The YMCA sponsored a boys' club in Oberlin both to help the boys and to prepare its own members for careers in city YMCA's.[30] It brought many speakers to the campus who discussed social issues and urged the members to pursue careers of social service. George A. Bellamy, for example, founder and director of the Hiram House social settlement in Cleveland, spoke on "The College Man in Social Settlement Work," outlining the "social, moral, political and religious conditions of the crowded tenement portions of Cleveland, and [giving] an . . . idea of the work done by Hiram Settlement, including a strong appeal to College men to investigate crowded cities."[31] Augustus K. Nash, the director of religious work for the Cleveland YMCA, spoke in 1904 to the Association on vocations for college men. The *Oberlin Review* recounted his appeal to the students to consider a career in social service:

> Usually when a man thinks of giving his life to the service of God he thinks of . . . becoming a minister or foreign missionary. Mr. Nash said that he believed the greatest opportunities for Christian work to-day are found among the industrial classes and the man who can take his place among these people . . . as one who is interested in the welfare of his fellowmen . . . [and] who has the power of leadership . . . has an opportunity for the largest Christian service.[32]

Jacob Riis, Judge Ben Lindsey, and Sophonisba Breckinridge were others with a commitment to humanitarian social reform who spoke to YMCA and YWCA audiences.[33] Simon MacLennan, professor of philosophy at Oberlin after the turn of the century, pointed out to the Association's members that at one time the YMCA's, like the churches, dealt with men strictly as individuals. Recently, however, "the center of interest has shifted to training for social welfare. . . . " He argued that "the religion of Christ was really democracy, and that all religion as well as all government should be by the people and for the people." [34] MacLennan urged the members to throw themselves into the struggle for a more perfect democracy.

The YMCA's encouraged the study of social themes in their Bible study courses. Courses in individual religious development naturally were still offered. Manuals for these courses, used at Oberlin and elsewhere, were written by Edward I. Bosworth, professor of New Testament language and literature in the Oberlin theological seminary. One of the most popular courses in the early twentieth century was that in "The Social Significance of the Teachings of Jesus," in which the manual by the Cornell University economist Jeremiah W. Jenks on *The Political and Social Significance of the Life and Teachings of Jesus* was used.[35] Jenks expressed his point of view in the preface where he wrote that as a student of politics and economics he had "taken a very great interest in seeing how the teachings which Jesus applied in his own life fit themselves into the lives and practices of the best thinkers of the present day . . . so that they are surely, although too slowly, regenerating the world." [36] The book included comments and questions on such topics as Jesus' teachings on wealth, his attitude toward the poor, and his principles of social reform. The popularity of this course among Oberlin men prompted a secretary of the college YMCA to write in 1908: "It does seem good to see men who come to Oberlin without ideas go out into the world not only with high ideals but knowledge of practical methods of Christianity, and fellow-service. And they make use of this knowledge too."[37]

The services of another agency of traditional evangelicalism, the Day of Prayer for Colleges, which sometimes stretched out to an entire week, were turned more frequently and to a greater extent to serve the needs of social redemption. Some students and many members of the faculty continued to view the Day of Prayer as primarily an opportunity for individualistic evangelicalism. Classes were suspended to reduce worldly distractions to the minimum. President King and other college officials sought to make the services an occasion for conversion and the profession of faith.[38] A veteran teacher described a meeting in 1904 as "quite like those of Pres. Finney's day."[39] At these times some students put time and energy into personal evangelical efforts. John G. Olmstead described his own evangelical work with some satisfaction: "It did me good to have one fellow, for whom I have for some time indirectly been working and the past week directly, take a stand for what he knew was right."[40] A teacher, who had only recently joined the faculty, described the scenes at two meetings in 1905:

> Dr. King made a brief talk at one point in which he almost broke down. Then the meeting was thrown open for *testimonies*. I suppose 20 or 30 students spoke. It was remarkable with what spontaneity and freedom they spoke. . . . [At a later meeting] a dozen men stood up to profess Christ, among them [the] Capt. of the Football Team next year. How these scenes bring back my old Princeton days.[41]

Despite these reports of enthusiastic and earnest meetings, scattered signs indicated a growing measure of student indifference. In 1905, in an editorial urging attendance at the meetings, the editor of the *Oberlin Review* indicated that some proportion of "upper-classmen . . . assume toward the Day of Prayer for Colleges a certain *blasé* attitude of bored indulgence."[42] The following year it was reported that "the tone of the week was perhaps not as openly spiritual as in some of the years gone, but there was abundant opportunity for those who sought it to find help for living." [43] The College itself even began to permit outside events to distract from that concentration upon religious and spiritual welfare which had been thought necessary to insure the success of the Day of Prayer. In 1913, for example, permission was granted to the Union Library Association to schedule a lecture by the English poet Alfred Noyes during the week of the services. [44]

The value and relevance of the services increased, according to students, as a larger measure of social content was introduced. In 1909 the editor of the *Oberlin Review*, summing up the worth of the recently concluded services, wrote:

> It has been interesting to note the growing ethical spirit among our American colleges. That this spirit has become vital in its influence is seen in the insistent demand for the clarified vision in matters of social service, the belief in the unqualified importance of Bible Study, and the practical interest shaping itself along lines of local political betterment. The significance of the past week bears right in upon this wide-spread tendency. The sober facing of values which attach themselves to a man's life is sometimes provocative of a startling sense of former thoughtlessness and indifference to the 'final cause'—that which gives man his conviction of function and purpose, and embodies the ideal toward which he strives. [45]

The climax in this blend of evangelical tone with social gospel content was reached during the services in February and March, 1916, led by Raymond Robins, a social reformer from Chicago. His message was "based on the conviction that the Gospel of Jesus Christ is sufficient to solve the individual, social, economic, and political problems of the day." [46] According to one report, "the meetings were evangelistic, and the appeal was made on the basis of a social gospel, 'Live the Christian life to help your fellows.'" [47]

President King added a social aspect to his popular training class for Christian workers. Among his recommended questions for the study of biblical passages was: "What *similar situations in our modern life,* personal or social, call for the application of this teaching?" and his outlines of the training class's work show the large number of social gospel topics with which he dealt. [48]

Many of those evangelical practices which failed to lend themselves directly to the propagation of social Christianity were discontinued.

The rule requiring attendance at Sunday services was revoked in 1906, owing to the impossibility of obtaining voluntary compliance and the incongruity of compulsion.[49] In 1915 after a long debate Monday classes began to be scheduled, necessitating study on the Sabbath.[50] One professor claimed that even before the decision was made Sunday study had become the rule rather than the exception. He was amazed, he wrote, when one of his best students told him that she did more studying on Sunday than on any other day of the week.[51] The voluntary class prayer meetings disappeared in the first decade of the twentieth century.[52] Daily chapel was still required of college students, although a monitoring system had to be adopted in 1913 in order to curtail excessive absences.[53] In addition, a slight requirement in Bible study courses for freshmen and seniors still prevailed. Even these old standbys were affected by the needs of a new age. The required senior course in Bible, entitled "Christian Ethics and Christian Religion," was intended "to give the student some intelligent introduction to the chief moral, religious, and theological problems of our time; and to bring out the most important practical . . . inferences from a comprehensive survey of present day world conditions."[54]

In the early twentieth century the College sponsored the propagation of social gospel tenets in other ways. A steady stream of speakers from outside enlightened undergraduates and faculty in the duties which social Christianity imposed upon them. Washington Gladden, an old favorite, made almost regular lecture appearances, always addressing the student body on some facet of social responsibility and reform.[55] Thinkers, clergymen, social workers, journalists and politicians, such as Walter Rauschenbusch, Graham Taylor, Florence Kelly, Lincoln Steffens, Shailer Mathews, Sophonisba Breckinridge, Charles M. Sheldon, Charles A. Beard, Joseph W. Folk, and Robert M. La Follette, appeared under college or student organization auspices.[56] With socialist authors Jack London and John Spargo attracting large audiences and much attention when they spoke in behalf of their cause, there was a greater diversity than ever before in the views presented to students.[57] In 1912 the Congregational Brotherhood of America, the social service arm of the Congregationalist churches, held its annual convention at Oberlin. The theme, appropriate for Oberlin, was "Social Service and Personal Evangelism," and the list of speakers included Gladden, George L. Cady, Edward

I. Bosworth, Hubert C. Herring, Owen R. Lovejoy, and Raymond Robins.[58]

Oberlin impressed many national leaders of the reform movement with the strength of its commitment to social Christianity. Walter Rauschenbusch and Josiah Strong sent their children to the College. They and others commented upon the intellectual vigor and social idealism of Oberlin students.[59] Theodore Roosevelt, pausing briefly in Oberlin during his campaign in the Ohio presidential preference primary of 1912, made political capital and paid tribute to the College and town when he said: "This is the community of the applied square deal. . . . What I preach you put in practice."[60] Oberlin Republicans repaid the compliment with their votes, giving Roosevelt better than a two-to-one majority in the primary.[61]

The study of the social sciences was even more closely tied to the needs of social reform than had earlier been the case. Albert B. Wolfe, professor of economics and sociology from 1905 to 1914, and one of the most popular teachers of his day, insisted that collegiate education should have a "social focus."[62] In urging a larger place for the social sciences in the curriculum, he argued that they provided the best foundation for higher learning:

> Young men today recognize quickly how much the country has for them to do, they have caught something of the social, as contra-distinct to the individualist spirit, and they are unwilling to spend four of the best years of life in attaining a purely individual culture. This situation the college must meet. If it meets it rightly, the place of the college in America will be greater than ever; if it does not, there will be a very great loss, not only to the colleges, which is a secondary matter, but to the social well-being, which should be the colleges' main concern.[63]

Wolfe thought that the study of sociology and economics was especially valuable in "backing up the traditional Oberlin idealism with a firmer foundation, in a harder-headed knowledge of social facts, and in affording opportunity for concrete application of the ideals of the College."[64] Wolfe's colleagues in the social science departments from 1900 to World War I, such as Ernest L. Bogart and Herbert A. Miller, shared his view that study of their subject should lead to an analysis of society and its problems providing guidance in social improvement. With more courses offered and an augmented corps of teachers, the social science departments became a more effective force than they had ever been before.

The efforts of the faculty combined with the needs of the times produced a great outburst of student interest in social problems and reforms. Student orations and literary society programs most commonly dealt with such matters. Prize-winning orations on "Ruskin's Message to Our Age," "The Evolution of Conscience," "The Age of Isms," and "Industrial Peace" bespoke the renewed commitment to social reform and progress.[65] In the Home Oratorical Contest of 1912 all six entrants, including the first woman permitted to enter such a contest at Oberlin, spoke on topics of political and social reform, with all save one taking an advanced progressive position. The first-place oration was devoted to the need for a new national political party of reform, a need apparently met by the formation of the Progressive party later in the year.[66] Child labor, working women, sweat shops, the threat of the trusts, arbitration of industrial conflicts, trade unions, workmen's compensation, profit sharing, socialism, immigrant problems, and city government were the stuff of society debates.[67]

An Oberlin Civic Club, founded in 1907 to promote discussion of problems of city life and reform, held regular meetings for approximately a year, then disappeared, but came to life again in 1912 in affiliation with the Intercollegiate Civic League. This second incarnation of the club undertook investigations of the qualifications of candidates for local and county offices as a part of the political education of its members and as a public service.[68]

On the left of the political spectrum, an unsuccessful attempt was made in 1911 by a recent graduate to establish an Oberlin socialist club.[69] In 1915, Herbert A. Miller, professor of sociology, sparked a second attempt, and an Oberlin Socialism Discussion Club was formed with Winifred Rauschenbusch, daughter of the Christian Socialist theologian Walter Rauschenbusch, as its first president.[70] The club was affiliated with the Intercollegiate Socialist Society and brought such socialist writers and lecturers as John Spargo and Rose Pastor Stokes to Oberlin to address large audiences.[71] With the entrance of the United States into World War I, a group from the Socialist Club published a short-lived pacifist paper, *The Rational Patriot*, condemning American involvement.[72]

Fulfilling the commitment to social service and reform had become the principal educational objective of many Oberlin students. In 1916 a group of students summarized the college's impact in a letter to the *Oberlin Review*:

> Of the Oberlin graduate, by virtue of the tradition and heritage of his Alma Mater, the world confidently expects religious and social leadership. Oberlin is founded upon the doctrine of democracy and has for her cornerstone the ideal of social service to the age. It is safe to assert that no man enters her halls without becoming conscious of this fact, and that few men receive her degree without acquiring an attitude of mind which leads them to respond to this demand for service.[73]

President King traced some of the contemporary implications of the principle of reverence for personality in his book, *The Moral and Religious Challenge of Our Times*.[74] In the judgment of a careful student of the social gospel movement, this book was one of the most important works on the application of social Christianity written before 1913.[75] Published in 1911 as the progressive movement in the United States approached flood tide, it showed how neatly Oberlin's social gospel meshed with political and social progressivism. The rise of progressive reform, King believed, justified a hearty optimism. Through the whole range of private and social life he discerned a new sensitivity to the need for social justice which had in turn prompted a demand for practical political, economic, and social reform. The principle of reverence for personality could render invaluable service to this movement by leading toward a middle way of constructive reform, transcending "the old opposition between an atomic, nihilistic individualism and a swamping socialism."[76] This path led through "both cooperation or state action and individual initiative at every stage, and both under ethical guidance."[77] Cooperation through the state would be used "not to set aside individual initiative, but more perfectly to secure it—sedulously to preserve for the life of the community and nation the full contribution of each personality."[78]

To create a "truer democracy," such reforms were needed as the conservation of natural resources, strict public regulation of utilities, control and use of patents in the public interest, limitations on the antisocial power of monopoly, and checks upon the accumulation of wealth.[79] Most of the stupendous fortunes of the day resulted from benefits bestowed by the public upon individuals, such as the use and exploitation of natural resources, the protective tariff, unearned increment in land values, and monopoly.[80] The consequent unjust distribution of wealth inevitably bred discontent, fed a hatred of the rich, and destroyed the harmony of American society. Combination on one side had been met by combination on the other; neither monopolies nor unions customarily took the public welfare into account in pursuing their interests. These injustices, he held, were not the work of a single class of exploiters, although a single class was the major beneficiary, but of all who acquiesced in them. "The whole people have been largely at fault; and it is for the whole people to repent, and to turn from shortsightedness, and from individual and class selfishness, to a deep-going justice."[81]

The principle of reverence for personality prescribed that the rights of persons should take precedence over the privileges of property. The establishment of personal rights called for some general reforms. The people had to recover control of the government. The control of national and state legislation by business interests had resulted in enormous abuses from high tariffs; the prevention of the passage of protective legislation for working men, children, and women; the wasteful exploitation of natural resources; and the failure to protect consumers from adulterated and diseased foods. "Commercial interests have been so dominant that legislation has been very largely a series of compromises between the various business interests of different sections; and the large problems concerning the welfare of the people as a whole have been grossly neglected."[82] Particular economic abuses, such as stock watering, the control of many corporations by a few men, and charging all that the traffic would bear, could be ended if a "consistently democratic national policy" were followed. King urged the passage of effective legislation to eliminate harsh working conditions and the adoption of orderly arbitration procedures to replace the anarchic industrial warfare of strikes. In the end, he believed, both capital and labor would profit from "such absolute community control; for they are engaged in a great common task, and all are indissolubly knit up in the fabric of one national life, where one cannot suffer and not all the rest suffer at the same time."[83] Like many Progressives, he thought that collective means could be fashioned that would meet individual needs and potentialities in an industrial era. The future, he believed, belonged to a "socialized individualism," offering the greatest opportunity for personal development.[84] With high hopes King wrote:

> When the spirit of reverence for personality thoroughly permeates all policies and all conduct, and is accompanied by scientific study of conditions, neither the individual nor the nation can fail. . . . For such a triumph deep religious conviction is necessary. For democracy is both an ideal and a faith. The honest, earnest, unselfish pursuit of a democracy, thus everywhere reverent of personality—even long before its fulfillment—would bring healing and health to our national life [and] enable it to render by example its largest possible service to the world's civilization.[85]

Most encouraging, King believed, was that rapid rise in "moral standards in the United States in business, industrial and political life" that had culminated in the progressive movement.[86] Oberlin, in seeking a new basis for service, had been working for this goal. The elevation of moral standards throughout collective and individual life, which King and others discerned, was due in some small part to those earnest teachers who had labored over the years to fit their students for worthy service. Generations of students had departed from college filled with a zeal for bettering the life of mankind as the highest expression of religious duty.

The movement for social, economic, and political reform of the early twentieth century bore many marks of its birth in a religious and academic matrix. In its constant moralizing, rather easy optimism, concern for the possibilities of individual development, striving after social harmony, moderation in particular reforms, and reliance upon the careful study of social conditions as the first step toward improvement, it reflected many of the same social, religious, and academic assumptions that shaped education at Oberlin. One source of the new progressivism was the old evangelical spirit, transmitted through the colleges and refashioned in the transition from an agrarian to an industrialized, bureaucratized, urban society.

The ease with which a progressive commitment evolved at Oberlin bears witness to the affinity between evangelicalism and progressivism. Without controversy, bitterness, friction, or charges of betrayal, the College passed from a preoccupation with the salvation of the soul to a determination to reform society. Through a middle-ground liberal theology, support for progressive politics, high standards of academic training with a social service goal governing instruction in the social sciences, and a variety of extracurricular activities of a social service nature, Oberlin forged a relationship with contemporary society that compared in relevance and vitality with the era of the antislavery crusade and Finney's revivals.

The new progressivism differed from its evangelical ancestor in other respects, since it was not so pervasive as a formative principle of college activities and policies. More nearly like other institutions of learning than formerly, Oberlin reflected the shifting pressures of a pluralistic social environment. The rise of organized athletics, the greater prominence and autonomy of the fine arts, and even, among some students, a concern with the superficial niceties of polite society, all reveal a fragmentation of student interests as well as, paradoxically, a search for common values and experiences. The religious and social progressivism which had become the representative faith of Oberlin was not, then, as inclusive of total student and faculty experiences as evangelicalism had been when at its height. This loss of unity had a positive value. If it made definition more difficult and diffused the impact of the College on society and students, it also created an opportunity for greater personal freedom. The partial liberalization of college life through the relaxation of social, religious, and intellectual restrictions, was a motif in Oberlin's history in this period, although college officials clung to the hope that the restraints of righteous living which no longer could be ensured through regulation might result from choice. Until the disruption attending American involvement in World War I produced powerful pressures for greater personal freedom, they largely succeeded.

Much of the zeal that had once gone into the advancement of evangelicalism was redirected to the pursuit of learning. Knowledge became the object of a determined quest, its possession the fulfillment of a moral obligation. Learning, still formally subordinate to a higher end, substantially enlarged its domain within the broad confines of social redemption. A greater intellectual sophistication and realism modified the idealistic innocence of old Oberlin. Indeed, the process of learning was gradually acquiring an autonomy that might, in time, break the Progressive synthesis of righteousness, social service, and scholarship. Still officially contained within assumptions of Christian thought and faith, the dynamics of learning and the mind gave no guarantee that they would always remain within that framework.

# NOTES

1. An exhaustive account of the history of early Oberlin, and a work on which I have steadily relied, is Robert S. Fletcher's *A History of Oberlin College from Its Foundation through the Civil War* (2 vols.; Oberlin: Oberlin College, 1943). The name Oberlin College was adopted in 1851.

2. The most thorough account of the history of American higher education is Frederick Rudolph, *The American College and University: A History* (New York: Alfred A. Knopf, 1962). A reconstruction of the academic milieu of Oberlin's early years is on pages 44–220.

3. The fullest treatment of Oberlin perfectionism is to be found in James William Lee, "The Development of Theology at Oberlin" (Ph.D. dissertation, Drew Theological Seminary, 1952), pp. 8–28. See also Timothy L. Smith, *Revivalism and Social Reform in Mid-Nineteenth Century America* (New York and Nashville: Abingdon Press, 1957), pp. 103–13.

4. Finney's views on reform—moral, political, social, and economic—and his understanding of the relationship between revivalism and reform are discussed in Charles C. Cole, Jr., *The Social Ideas of the Northern Evangelists, 1826–1860* (New York: Columbia University Press, 1954).

5. For a recollection of the Oberlin spirit during the sixties, which the author thought was unique, see Denton Jacques Snider, *A Writer of Books in His Genesis* (St. Louis: Sigma Publishing Co., n.d.), p. 157.

6. For a sketch of Fairchild's life and theological ideas, see the article by Edward Dwight Eaton in the *Dictionary of American Biography*. A far more extensive but very uneven account is that of Albert T. Swing, *James Harris Fairchild* (New York: Fleming H. Revell Co., 1907).

7. "Journal of Professor Lyman B. Hall" (Oberlin College Library), III, 182; Alfred V. Churchill, "Midwestern: Early Oberlin Personalities," *Northwest Ohio Quarterly*, XXIII, No. 4 (Autumn, 1951), 212; Alfred V. Churchill, "Midwestern: Transition at Oberlin, 1850–1887," *ibid.*, XXIV, No. 4 (Autumn, 1952), 228–32; Swing, pp. 189, 195–96, 199–202, 204–5; Charles B. Martin, "Reminiscences of Charles B. Martin" (Mimeographed, Oberlin College Library), p. 15.

8. James Harris Fairchild, *Oberlin: The Colony and the College, 1833–1883* (Oberlin: E. J. Goodrich, 1883).

9. Churchill, "Midwestern: Transition at Oberlin, 1850–1887," pp. 231–32.

10. [Delavan L. Leonard], "Notes of Talks with President Fairchild, No. 1, December 20, 1894–November 16, 1897" (Oberlin College Library), pp. 85–86. Leonard's contractions in his notes have been expanded in the textual quotation.

11. Quoted in Swing, p. 53.

12. *Ibid.* See the outline of a sermon on the text, "But one sinner destroyeth much good," Eccl. 9:18, *ibid.*, 178–83, which Swing states was "as near an approach to a revival sermon as President Fairchild ever made." It is a far cry from Finney's sermons.

13. The best study of the Oberlin theological tradition is Lee, "The Development of Theology at Oberlin." See Winthrop S. Hudson, *American Protestantism* (Chicago: University of Chicago Press, 1961), pp. 29–33, 74–102, for a brief but stimulating introduction to the origin of evangelical Protestantism in America. Hudson's work should be read within the more general interpretive context of Sidney E. Mead's article, "Denominationalism: The Shape of Protestantism in America," *Church History*, XXIII, No. 4 (December, 1954), 291–320.

14. James Harris Fairchild, *Elements of Theology, Natural and Revealed* (Oberlin: E. J. Goodrich, 1892). A list of Fairchild's writings on religious, educational, and historical subjects, mostly published in periodicals, is in Swing, pp. 393–96.

15. Frank Hugh Foster, *A Genetic History of the New England Theology* (Chicago: University of Chicago Press, 1907), p. 469.

16. This address was printed in full in the *Oberlin News*, October 15, 1874.

17. See the letters of Rev. H. B. Fry and Gen. A. B. Nettleton to Fairchild, printed in Swing, p. 202, 382.

18. Churchill, "Midwestern: Transition at Oberlin, 1850–1887," p. 232. He did, however, carry on a large private correspondence on religious questions, judging from the number of letters he received on such matters. See James Harris Fairchild Papers (Oberlin College Library). Cited hereafter as Fairchild Papers.

19. James Harris Fairchild, *Educational Arrangements and College Life at Oberlin* (New York: Edward O. Jenkins, 1866). It was delivered at Commencement, August 22, 1866.

20. *Ibid.*, p. 8.

21. For the continuing ethical preoccupation of Oberlin theology, which came close to making religion a means for the achievement of moral ends, see Lee, pp. 113–23.

22. Fairchild, *Educational Arrangements and College Life at Oberlin*, p. 11.

23. *Oberlin Review*, August 1, 1877.

24. Leonard, pp. 105, 107. Leonard's contractions have been expanded.

25. *Ibid.*, p. 106.

26. Swing, pp. 146–47.

27. The preparatory department closed its doors in 1916; the theological seminary was ordered closed by the board of trustees in 1965.

28. Fairchild, *Educational Arrangements and College Life at Oberlin*, p. 20.

29. *Ibid.*

30. For an informed survey of these developments, see Rudolph, pp. 264–306, 329–54.

31. The establishment of the principle of faculty control over academic policy is discussed in Fletcher, I, 168–70. See also the comments of Mrs. Adelia A. F. Johnston, the Principal of the Ladies' Department, on Fairchild's adherence to the principle, quoted in Swing, p. 357.

32. The financial history may be most conveniently traced in the *Annual Reports of the President*.

33. His uneasiness before the strange and the new is revealed in the account of his European tour of 1870–71 in Swing, p. 238.

34. *Ibid.*, pp. 210–11.

35. Delavan L. Leonard, *The Story of Oberlin: The Institution, the Community, the Idea, the Movement* (Boston: Pilgrim Press, 1898), pp. 339-61; Williston Walker, *A History of the Congregational Churches in the United States* (New York: Charles Scribner's Sons, 1916), pp. 361-65, 371.

36. Fletcher, I, 177-78.

37. Information on the trustees has been gathered from a list published under the title *Oberlin College, Alumni Register: Graduates and Former Students, Teaching and Administrative Staff, 1833-1960* (Oberlin: Oberlin College, 1960), Int. 21-56, cited hereafter as *Oberlin College, Alumni Register;* and from Fletcher, *passim.*

38. The nine faculty members and their subjects in 1866 were: George N. Allen, professor of geology and natural history; Charles H. Churchill, professor of mathematics and natural philosophy; James Dascomb, professor of chemistry, botany and physiology; John M. Ellis, professor of mental philosophy and rhetoric; James H. Fairchild, professor of moral philosophy; Charles H. Penfield, professor of Greek; Giles W. Shurtleff, adjunct professor of Latin; Judson Smith, professor of Latin; James A. Thome, instructor in elocution. Thome was also a trustee. See *Oberlin College, Alumni Register,* Int. 21-52. Comments on most of these men and their teaching may be found in Fletcher, *passim.*

In addition to those listed there were teachers for students in music, theology, and the college preparatory department. The women in the Literary Course also had, in part, a separate faculty. Since this study deals only with the liberal arts college and not with Oberlin in all of its branches, they have been omitted.

39. The five were Allen, Ellis, Fairchild, Penfield, and Shurtleff.

40. Churchill was a graduate of Dartmouth. Although Smith attended Amherst College during his senior year and was graduated there, he received the rest of his undergraduate instruction at Oberlin.

41. For comments on this practice in other American colleges of the day, see Rudolph, pp. 159-60.

42. For an analysis of the financing of nineteenth century higher education, see Frederick Rudolph, "Who Paid the Bills?" *Harvard Educational Review,* XXXI, No. 2 (Spring, 1961), 152-57.

43. For example, see Fairchild's remarks in the "Annual Report of the President for 1876," printed in the *Oberlin News,* August 3, 1876.

44. *Oberlin Review,* March 5, 1881.

45. "Journal of Professor Lyman B. Hall," I, 44.

46. Biographical data is in Fletcher, II, 691-92. A picture of Ellis taken in 1859 is reproduced opposite p. 692. See also *A Tribute to the Memory of John Millott Ellis, D.D.* (Oberlin; Pearce and Randolph, 1894).

47. John M. Ellis, *Oberlin and the American Conflict* (Oberlin: Oberlin News, 1865).

48. See his article, "Have We Too Many Colleges?" *Oberlin Review,* July 8, 1874.

49. Henry N. Castle to "Dear Folks at Home," May 24, 1882; Henry N. Castle to parents, October 13, 1882; November 4, 1882; February 3, 1883, Henry N. Castle Papers (University of Chicago Library). Cited hereafter as Castle Papers.

50. Further discussion of the selection of a president in 1889–1891 is on pp. 69–71.

51. Biographical information is in Fletcher, II, 629, 692, 789-90, 801, 805, 897, 903. The reproduction of a photograph from the 1859 Class Album faces p. 692.

52. Martin, p. 18; "Diary of May L. Goldsbury" (Oberlin College Library), p. 1.

53. See, for example, Martin, pp. 83-84.

54. *Annual Report of the President for 1881*, p. 6.

55. Robert A. Millikan, *The Autobiography of Robert A. Millikan* (New York: Prentice-Hall, 1950), pp. 14-15, 17.

56. R. T. Miller, Jr., to Henry C. King, May 21, 1913, Henry Churchill King Papers (Oberlin College Library). Cited hereafter as King Papers.

57. Alfred V. Churchill, "Midwestern: Professor Charles Henry Churchill of Oberlin," *Northwest Ohio Quarterly*, XXIV, No. 3 (Summer, 1952), 148-50, 153.

58. *Ibid.*, p. 148.

59. *Ibid.*, p. 147; Alfred V. Churchill, "Midwestern: An Oberlin Family," *ibid.*, XXVII, No. 4 (Autumn, 1955), 181-82. See also the manuscript by Archer H. Shaw, "Charles Henry Churchill" (Oberlin College Library), and the sketch by George F. Wright in the *Oberlin Review*, June 23, 1897.

60. Churchill, "Midwestern: Transition at Oberlin, 1850-1887," pp. 233-35.

61. See his article "College Prizes," *Oberlin Review*, March 22, 1876.

62. For brief descriptions and characterizations of a number of Oberlin teachers, see Martin, pp. 18-22.

63. Statement from an oration of Cook's entitled "The Teachings of Plymouth Rock," quoted in the *Annual Report of the President for 1880*, pp. 10-11.

64. See Alfred V. Churchill, "Midwestern: Oberlin Students, Sinners and Adolescents in the 1870's and 1880's," *Northwest Ohio Quarterly*, XXV, No. 1 (Winter, 1953), 41.

65. In addition seventeen women received diplomas for completion of the Literary Course, which did not include Greek or as much science as the Classical Course.

66. Figures on the geographical and social background of the members of the class are taken from a survey published in the *Oberlin Review*, August 4, 1875.

67. *Ibid.*, May 24, 1876.

68. *Ibid.*, April 8, 1882. One member of the class had died. For a statistical study of the vocational choices of Oberlin students between 1877 and 1926, see L. D. Hartson, "The Occupations Which College Graduates Enter," *Vocational Guidance Magazine*, VI, No. 7 (April, 1928), 297-302. For a study of the life of one distinguished member of the class, the Negro scholar and educator William Sanders Scarborough, see Francis P. Weisenburger, "William Sanders Scarborough: Early Life and Years at Wilberforce," *Ohio History*, LXXI, No. 3 (October, 1962), 203-26, and "William Sanders Scarborough: Scholarship, the Negro, Religion, and Politics," *ibid.*, LXXII, No. 1 (January, 1963), 25-50.

69. See the interesting, though incomplete, comparison of occupational intentions of the class of 1875 at Oberlin, Harvard, Yale, Princeton, Amherst, Lafayette, the University of Michigan, and Cornell University in the *Oberlin Review*, May 24, 1876. Of these institutions, only Amherst approached and none equalled or surpassed Oberlin in the percentage of its graduates who planned to enter the ministry.

70. A great outpouring of political enthusiasm came in 1880 when James A. Garfield was elected to the presidency. After celebrations in Oberlin a train was chartered to carry students, faculty, and townspeople to the victorious candidate's home in Mentor, Ohio, where felicitous greetings were exchanged. The celebration was described by President Fairchild in his report for the year. An interesting account is contained in the letter of Henry N. Castle to "Dear Folks in General," November 9, 1880, Castle Papers.

71. See, for example, the comparisons in the *Oberlin Review*, October 23, 1878.

72. *Ibid.*, August 4, 1875. For similar figures on later classes, see *ibid.*, June 27, 1885, June 28, 1887. Comparable figures for New England colleges, which

also illustrate the homogeneity of the student body, are given in George E. Peterson, *The New England College in the Age of the University* (Amherst, Mass.: Amherst College Press, 1964), pp. 77–79.

73. See, for example, the statement of Fairchild in the *Annual Report of the President for 1886*, p. 2.

74. A thorough discussion of this is in Fletcher, I, 124–26 ff., II, 634 ff.

75. See, for example, the letter of Freeman Walker to James H. Fairchild, June 28, 1883, Fairchild Papers.

76. *Oberlin Review*, March 11, 1882.

77. *Ibid.*, August 2, 1875.

78. *Ibid.*, May 24, 1876.

79. *Catalogue of Oberlin College, 1884–1885*, p. 74.

80. Churchill, "Midwestern: Transition at Oberlin, 1850–1887," pp. 221.

81. *Oberlin Review*, June 23, 1875.

82. Trustees' Minutes, July 27, 1877.

83. *Catalogue of Oberlin College, 1884–1885*, p. 72.

84. *Catalogue of Oberlin College, 1877–1878*, p. 47.

85. Compiled from various sources. See *ibid.*, pp. 47–48; *Oberlin Review*, February 24, 1875; May 19, 1875; September 22, 1875; February 23, 1876; May 24, 1876; September 27, 1876; September 19, 1877; March 19, 1879; October 10, 1885.

86. *Oberlin Review*, April 14, 1883.

87. *Ibid.*, April 15, 1874. The student newspaper always reported society programs.

88. *Ibid.*, May 13, 1874.

89. *Ibid.*, September 19, 1877.

90. For an historical account by the Rev. Henry Matson of the founding and the work of the Union Library Association, see *ibid.*, May 16, 1894.

91. *Catalogue of Oberlin College, 1884–1885*, pp. 70–72.

92. Martin, p. 26.

93. For an amusing account of Oberlin courting, see Margaret W. Eggleston (ed.), *Kathie's Diary* (New York: George H. Doran Co., 1926), p. 272. The author of the diary and letters published in this work is anonymous, but they are probably authentic.

94. Alfred V. Churchill, "Midwestern: Scientific and Musical Beginnings at Oberlin," *Northwest Ohio Quarterly*, XXIV, No. 2 (Spring, 1952), 109.

95. A. L. Shumway and C. De W. Brower (eds.), *Oberliniana: A Jubilee Volume of Semi-Historical Anecdotes Connected with the Past and Present of Oberlin College* (Cleveland: Home Publishing Co., [1883]), pp. 90–91.

96. *Oberlin Review*, July 5, 1876.

97. Martin, p. 23.

98. Mrs. Johnston dominated the women of the College and was an important influence in many other ways for more than twenty-five years. Besides ruling the Ladies' Department she taught history in the Literary Course. For sympathetic accounts, see Harriet L. Keeler, *The Life of Adelia A. Field Johnston* (Cleveland: Korner and Wood Co., 1912), and Frances J. Hosford, *Father Shipherd's Magna Charta: A Century of Coeducation in Oberlin College* (Boston: Marshall Jones Co., 1937), pp. 139–64. See also Martin, p. 19.

99. Original in the Fairchild Papers, dated June 28, 1881. See also the *Catalogue of Oberlin College, 1884–1885*, p. 72.

100. See the *Oberlin Review*, March 8, 1876.

101. See, for example, the letter of Mrs. Mary B. Shurtleff, a member of the Ladies' Board, to Professor Giles W. Shurtleff, May 1, 1877, Giles W. Shurtleff Papers (Oberlin College Library). Cited hereafter as Shurtleff Papers.

102. See the exchange of opinions in the *Oberlin Review*, July 19, 1876; September 13, 1876; September 27, 1876; December 20, 1876; and the editorial on student acceptance of the rules in *ibid.*, March 20, 1878.

103. *Oberlin News*, November 15, 1878; *Oberlin Review*, November 20, 1878, January 22, 1879. There are a number of letters in the Fairchild Papers on this incident.

104. As only two of many examples, see the *Oberlin Review*, October 6, 1875; February 23, 1876.

105. Agnes Fairchild to James T. Fairchild, January 1, 1881, Fairchild Papers.

106. There is a considerable literature of alumni reminiscence on social life and the rules. See Dan F. Bradley, "Between Classes," *Oberlin Alumni Magazine*, XXIX, No. 10 (July, 1933), 297–300; Dan F. Bradley, "Then and Now," *ibid.*, XXVIII, No. 3 (December, 1931), 71–72; Arthur T. Burrell, "Oberlin Social Life in the Seventies," *ibid.*, XXVIII, No. 1 (October, 1931), 8–9; Alfred V. Churchill, "Midwestern: Oberlin Students, Sinners and Adolescents in the 1870's and 1880's," pp. 41–62; Martin, p. 24. See also the historical article by Robert Samuel Fletcher, "Horse and Buggy Days," *Oberlin Alumni Magazine*, XLVII, No. 1 (November, 1950), 4–5, 11.

107. *Catalogue of Oberlin College, 1884–1885*, p. 64; *Catalogue of Oberlin College, 1888–1889*, p. 88. For general accounts of Oberlin religious life, see Leonard, *The Story of Oberlin*, pp. 404–6; Keeler, pp. 79–80; and the mixture of fact and fancy in L. L. Jones, *Oberlin and Eastern School Life* (Warren, Ohio: Trumbull Printing Co., 1889), pp. 145–68. For student notes in one course, see Anna M. Metcalf, "Notes on Professor John M. Ellis' Course, Evidences of Christianity, Spring, 1882," (Oberlin College Library).

108. *Oberlin Review*, October 17, 1877.

109. For a description, see "Robert" [Robert S. Lindsay] to Mrs. Dove, September 19, 1877, George Frederick Wright Papers (Oberlin College Library). Cited hereafter as G. F. Wright Papers.

110. *Catalogue of Oberlin College, 1884–1885*, p. 70.

111. *Oberlin Review*, May 26, 1883.

112. Keeler, p. 80.

113. "Robert" [Robert S. Lindsay] to Mrs. Dove, September 19, 1877, G. F. Wright Papers.

114. In 1879 the editors claimed that fully one-half of the college newspapers they received through exchange contained some comment on this Oberlin custom. *Oberlin Review*, October 16, 1879.

115. *Ibid.*, January 22, 1881.

116. *Ibid.*, November 3, 1875.

117. *Ibid.*

118. *Oberlin News*, December 11, 1873.

119. *Oberlin Review*, December 25, 1878.

120. William G. Frost, *For the Mountains, An Autobiography* (New York: Fleming H. Revell Co., 1937), pp. 46–47. See also Frost's article, "A Word in the Pastor's Absence," *Advance*, XVI, No. 729 (September 8, 1881), 562–63. For Mrs. Johnston's conduct of the Young Ladies' Prayer Meeting, see Keeler, pp. 166–70. For some candid comments on topics, methods, student participation,

and the teacher's effectiveness, see the "Journal of Professor Lyman B. Hall," I, 4, 8–9, 31, 34–36, 40–41, 43–48, 51, 54–55, 62, 64, 66, 109, 146, 154, 202.

121. *Oberlin Review*, April 18, 1885.

122. C. Howard Hopkins, *History of the Y.M.C.A. in North America* (New York: Association Press, 1951), pp. 271–83.

123. See the *Oberlin Review*, May 28, 1881, June 11, 1881, November 26, 1881, December 10, 1881.

124. *Ibid.*, February 25, 1882.

125. See Hopkins, pp. 292–93.

126. *Oberlin Review*, December 1, 1883.

127. For a historical account, see Florence M. Fitch, "President King's Training Class," *Oberlin Alumni Magazine*, IV, No. 2 (November, 1907), 38–40.

128. *Oberlin Review*, May 1, 1895.

129. See, for example, the account in *ibid.*, February 3, 1883; "Journal of Professor Lyman B. Hall," I, 44, 115, 207.

130. Shumway and Brower, pp. 54–55.

131. *Oberlin Review*, January 24, 1877.

132. Mary Wright to Mr. and Mrs. Albert A. Wright, February 7, 1877, Albert A. Wright Papers (Oberlin College Library). Cited hereafter as A. A. Wright Papers.

133. *Ibid.*; *Oberlin Review*, March 14, 1877.

134. James K. Newton to his mother, February 3, 1879, Abel Newton Papers (State Historical Society of Wisconsin). Cited hereafter as Newton Papers.

135. Henry N. Castle to "Dear Sister Hattie," February 6, 1879, Castle Papers. See also the *Oberlin Review*, February 5, 1879, February 19, 1879.

136. *Annual Report of the President for 1879*, p. 2.

137. *Annual Report of the President for 1880*, p. 2.

138. The figures are for male graduates who were living in 1926 when the survey was made. Hartson, p. 301. For Oberlin's support of foreign missions, see Leonard, *The Story of Oberlin*, pp. 316–38.

139. "Kathie" to her mother, 1881. Printed in Eggleston, p. 217.

140. Accounts of Oberlin's missionary activities in the nineteenth century are to be found in Leonard, *The Story of Oberlin*, pp. 323–38, and Fairchild, *Oberlin: The Colony and the College*, pp. 133–53. Certain aspects of this work during the ante bellum period are treated exhaustively by Fletcher in *A History of Oberlin College, passim*.

141. *Ibid.*, I, 259 f., and references cited there.

142. Leonard, *The Story of Oberlin*, p. 336.

143. *Ibid.*, p. 305.

144. A summary of local temperance activities in the late nineteenth century may be found in *ibid.*, pp. 304–7. Fletcher's *A History of Oberlin College*, I, 336–40, contains information on ante bellum temperance societies and activities.

145. *Oberlin Review*, September 17, 1881, for an extensive account. See also the "Record Book of the Oberlin Temperance Alliance," (Oberlin College Library), I, 180 ff.; Shumway and Brower, p. 167.

146. *Oberlin Review*, September 17, 1881.

147. Shumway and Brower, pp. 164–65.

148. *Oberlin Review*, September 17, 1881; "Record Book of the Oberlin Temperance Alliance," I, 180.

149. *Oberlin Review,* January 7, 1882, January 21, 1882.

150. *Ibid.,* February 4, 1882.

151. *Ibid.,* February 25, 1882. See also Shumway and Brower, pp. 163–65; "Record Book of the Oberlin Temperance Alliance," I, 159.

152. *Oberlin Review,* March 11, 1882; *The Whole Story: History of the Oberlin Temperance War, 1882* (Cleveland: Leader Printing Co., 1882).

153. "Record Book of the Oberlin Temperance Alliance," I, 196.

154. *Oberlin Review,* April 8, 1882.

155. *Catalogue of Oberlin College, 1884–1885,* p. 75.

156. For a contemporary statement of "Oberlin's Ideal," see the article so entitled by the Rev. Henry Matson in the *Oberlin Review,* April 21, 1875.

157. Very rarely it was charged that racial discrimination was practiced by some students. Such charges were always officially denied. The evidence that the author has been able to uncover is inconclusive. It seems likely that the official claim of non-discriminatory acceptance of Negroes was substantially true, although instances of discrimination did occasionally occur. See scattered letters in the Fairchild papers, 1882–1884; the *Oberlin Review,* February 3, 1883 and March 3, 1883; Eggleston, pp. 222–25, 229; and the letter of Henry N. Castle to his mother and sister on January 2, 1883, Castle Papers.

## CHAPTER II

1. For commentary on the universities impact on the colleges see Rudolph, *The American College,* pp. 241–306. A superb collection of documents on the history of the university in the United States is Volume II of Richard Hofstadter and Wilson Smith (eds.), *American Higher Education: A Documentary History* (Chicago: University of Chicago Press, 1961). This work offers the best introduction to the various issues generated by the rise of universities. There is also much pertinent material in the broadly conceived work of Richard Hofstadter and Walter P. Metzger, *The Development of Academic Freedom in the United States* (New York: Columbia University Press, 1955), and in Laurence R. Veysey, *The Emergence of the American University* (Chicago: University of Chicago Press, 1965).

2. Trustees' Minutes, June 8, 1878, March 5, 1890.

3. See, for example, Lucien C. Warner, *Personal Memoirs of L. C. Warner* (New York: Association Press, 1915). Warner, an Oberlin graduate in the Class of 1865, was a leading member of the board from 1873 to 1925, a generous benefactor of both Oberlin and the YMCA, and a well-known East Coast manufacturer.

4. Trustees' Minutes, July 30, 1875, July 31, 1875.

5. *Oberlin College, Alumni Register,* Int. 21–56.

6. Following Fairchild's retirement in 1889 the fourteen members of the faculty who were teaching at least some college courses were: Edward I. Bosworth, professor of English Bible; William B. Chamberlain, professor of elocution; Charles H. Churchill, professor of mathematics and natural philosophy; John M. Ellis, professor of mental and moral philosophy; William G. Frost, professor of Greek; Lyman B. Hall, professor of Latin; Charles Harris, professor of German; Frank F. Jewett, professor of chemistry; Henry C. King, associate professor of mathematics; Charles B.

Martin, assistant professor of Latin and Greek; James Monroe, professor of political science and modern history; Harry H. Powers, professor of French; Elmer H. Stanley, instructor in mathematics; Albert A. Wright, professor of geology and natural history.

7. See *Oberlin College, Alumni Register*, Int. 21–56. Frank H. Foster, professor of church history since 1884, also had a Leipzig Ph.D., but since he taught exclusively in the theological seminary he is outside the scope of this study. See Rudolph, *The American College*, pp. 395–96, for comments and some illustrative figures on the influx of Ph.D.'s. Oberlin lagged well behind the East Coast colleges in this respect.

8. Dan F. Bradley to James H. Fairchild, June 19, 1888, Fairchild Papers.

9. William G. Frost to Lyman B. Hall, April 25 [?], 1889, Lyman B. Hall Papers (Oberlin College Library). Cited hereafter as Hall Papers. For Frost's statement of the "foundation facts and principles" of Oberlin, see the account of his Thursday Lecture in the *Oberlin Review*, February 17, 1883. In 1892 he resigned his position at Oberlin to accept the presidency of Berea College. Some interesting letters he wrote to President Henry C. King between 1907 and 1916, lamenting the passing of the old Oberlin, are in the King Papers. For a later, personal impression, see the "Journal of Professor Kemper Fullerton" (Oberlin College Library), entry of February 24, 1905.

10. A letter of Frost's entitled "A Valedictory," written when he resigned from the Oberlin faculty, printed in the *Oberlin News*, September 15, 1892.

11. For example, see the letters of Giles Shurtleff to James H. Fairchild, February 9, 1887; Judson Smith to James H. Fairchild, January 29, 1885; Judson Smith to William G. Frost, January 3, 1887, Fairchild Papers.

12. *Oberlin Review*, October 7, 1874. For a similar article, see *ibid.*, February 4, 1882.

13. *Ibid.*, October 7, 1874. See also Churchill, "Midwestern: Transition at Oberlin, 1850–1887," pp. 233–35.

14. As one example, see the account of Henry C. King's work at Harvard University in Donald M. Love, *Henry Churchill King of Oberlin* (New Haven, Conn.: Yale University Press, 1956), pp. 25–42.

15. "Journal of Professor Lyman B. Hall," I, 147–49.

16. *Oberlin Review*, September 20, 1892.

17. Charles B. Martin to Lyman B. Hall, October, 1888 [?], Hall Papers.

18. "Journal of Professor Lyman B. Hall," II, 28; *Oberlin Review*, September 20, 1892.

19. *Ibid.*, May 3, 1892; "Journal of Professor Lyman B. Hall," II, 49. By the time he delivered this lecture Powers probably had decided to resign. See *Ibid.*, II, 30.

20. *Ibid.*, p. 49.

21. See his article, "An Important Step of Progress," *Oberlin Review*, March 31, 1891.

22. *Ibid.*, April 5, 1893.

23. *Ibid.*

24. *Ibid.*, January 11, 1887.

25. *Ibid.*, June 9, 1875.

26. *Ibid.*, March 28, 1877.

27. *Ibid.*

28. *Ibid.*, October 11, 1887.

29. *Ibid.*

30. *Ibid.*, March 6, 1888.

31. *Ibid.*, November 4, 1874.

32. *Ibid.*, November 4, 1874, March 24, 1875.

33. *Ibid.*, October 31, 1877.

34. *Ibid.*

35. *Ibid.*, April 30, 1879.

36. See especially the articles in *ibid.*, November 20, 1878, April 30, 1879, June 10, 1880, February 25, 1882, March 25, 1882.

37. See, for example, the letter from "E.S.S." [E. S. Steele] on Harvard, in *ibid.*, March 14, 1877.

38. *Ibid.*, March 4, 1880.

39. *Ibid.*, June 6, 1877.

40. *Ibid.*, March 19, 1881.

41. An enlightening study of Johns Hopkins is Hugh Hawkins, *Pioneer: A History of the Johns Hopkins University, 1874–1889* (Ithaca, N.Y.: Cornell University Press, 1960).

42. *Oberlin Review*, November 6, 1888. This information was confirmed by the graduate students' Register at Johns Hopkins University.

43. Toyokichi Iyenaga to James Monroe, November 26, 1887, James Monroe Papers (Oberlin College Library). Cited hereafter as Monroe Papers. For a full description of one Oberlin graduate's work at Johns Hopkins, see the letters of John R. Commons to James Monroe, January 4, 1888 [1889]; May 14, 1889; October 25, 1889; December 19, 1889; February 27, 1890; June 7, 1890, Monroe Papers.

44. See the *Oberlin Review*, February 15, 1887; May 28, 1889, for firsthand reports on Johns Hopkins by Oberlin alumni.

45. Eliot's address is printed in Charles W. Eliot, *Educational Reform: Essays and Addresses* (New York: Century Co., 1898), pp. 1-38. See also Rudolph, *The American College*, pp. 290-95.

46. Fletcher, *A History of Oberlin College*, I, 209, II, 694-95.

47. *Oberlin Review*, April 21, 1875; November 4, 1874; March 24, 1875.

48. Trustees' Minutes, July 30, 1875.

49. *Oberlin Review*, July 21, 1875; August 4, 1875.

50. *Catalogue of Oberlin College, 1885-1886*, p. 64.

51. *Annual Report of the President for 1885*, p. 2; "Journal of Professor Lyman B. Hall," I, 55; *Catalogue of Oberlin College 1885–1886*, pp. 64–66.

52. For required and elective courses in 1889, the year of Fairchild's retirement, see the *Catalogue of Oberlin College, 1889–1890*, pp. 31, 35–36. For a favorable estimate of electives at Oberlin, see Martin, p. 25.

53. For ante bellum instruction in modern foreign languages, see Fletcher, *A History of Oberlin College*, II, 723-25.

54. Trustees' Minutes, July 30, 1875. Newton had studied at Oberlin but did not graduate. He tells of his appointment and remarks on his teaching in three letters to his mother: August 8, 1875; October 8, 1877; February 3, 1879; Newton Papers.

55. See Martin, p. 19.

56. See the *Oberlin Review*, September 19, 1877.

57. "Journal of Professor Lyman B. Hall." I, 84.

58. *Annual Report of the President for 1887*, p. 3. John M. Ellis to Lyman B. Hall, November 12, 1888, Hall Papers. For a sketch of the formidable "Tutor Martin," see Eggleston, pp. 219-20.

59. *Oberlin Review*, October 9, 1880.

60. William G. Frost to James H. Fairchild, May 21, 1886, Fairchild Papers; William G. Frost to Lyman B. Hall, April [?], 1889, Hall Papers. See also the thoughtful student editorial on the value of studying the ancient classics as literature in the *Oberlin Review*, October 21, 1882.

61. *Annual Report of the President for 1888*, p. 5; "Journal of Professor Lyman B. Hall," I, 199.

62. See, for example, the editorial in the *Oberlin Review*, May 1, 1878.

63. *Ibid.*, November 6, 1878. Monthly Rhetoricals were abolished in 1887. For a description of this exercise, see the article by Etta M. Wright in *ibid.*, January 9, 1897.

64. *Ibid.*, October 29, 1881.

65. See, for example, the comments in *ibid.*, March 31, 1883.

66. *Annual Report of the President for 1880*, p. 8; *Annual Report for 1889, by the Chairman of the Faculty*, p. 7.

67. Henry N. Castle to "Dear Parents and All," February 25, 1883, Castle Papers.

68. See the article by B. H. Burtt in the form of a letter to the editor in the *Oberlin Review*, December 21, 1886, and the reply from another student, R. C. Martin, in defense of compulsory attendance, in *ibid.*, January 11, 1887.

69. Snider, pp. 108-09.

70. *Oberlin Review*, October 17, 1877; February 28, 1878.

71. *Ibid.*, April 14, 1883. For a similar statement, see *ibid.*, March 4, 1877.

72. *Ibid.*, April 14, 1883.

73. Swing, pp. 187-88.

74. *Ibid.*

75. *Oberlin Review*, October 11, 1876.

76. *Ibid.*

77. As examples, see the editorials in *ibid.*, May 14, 1879; May 28, 1881; October 21, 1882; November 4, 1882; January 6, 1883; March 17, 1883.

78. Charles B. Martin to Lyman B. Hall, November 23, 1885, Hall Papers. At the time Martin was studying philosophy, among other subjects, at the University of Berlin.

79. Martin, "Reminiscences of Charles B. Martin," p. 6.

80. Henry N. Castle to George H. Mead, June 29, 1883, Castle Papers.

81. Henry N. Castle to his parents, October 13, 1882, June 10, 1893, Castle Papers.

82. George H. Mead, "Recollections of Henry Northrup Castle in Oberlin, and After," in George and Helen Mead (eds.), *Henry Northrup Castle: Letters* (London: privately printed, 1902), pp. 807-12. This edition of Castle letters includes most of those now in the University of Chicago collection of Castle Papers.

83. Henry N. Castle to "Dear Folks at Home," May 24, 1882; October 13, 1882; November 4, 1882; February 3, 1883, Castle Papers.

84. Robert Lindsay to George F. Wright, May 21, 1880, G. F. Wright Papers.

85. See the *Oberlin Review*, December 11, 1879, and the acid comments in the letter of Henry N. Castle to his parents, February 3, 1883, Castle Papers.

86. Martin, "Reminiscences of Charles B. Martin," p. 18.

87. *Oberlin Review*, February 25, 1882; February 17, 1883; Henry N. Castle to "Dear Sister Hattie," May 1, 1883, Castle Papers.

88. *Oberlin Review*, January 10, 1885.

89. See, as examples of student opinion, the following essays or orations: *Oberlin Review*, April 29, 1874; June 24, 1874; October 21, 1874; July 7, 1875; November 17, 1875; September 19, 1877; November 28, 1877; February 5, 1880; November 18, 1882; October 20, 1883.

90. *Ibid.*, October 21, 1874; July 7, 1875.

91. Edward K. Fairchild, "Modern Iconoclasm," *ibid.*, February 23, 1876.

92. For a discussion of the identification in much Protestant thinking of evolution and moral progress, see Arthur C. McGiffert, *The Rise of Modern Religious Ideas* (New York: Macmillan Co., 1915), pp. 166-86.

93. *Oberlin Review*, October 25, 1876.

94. W. A. Gates, "Evolution and Free Will," *ibid.*, January 23, 1878.

95. L. W. Morris, "Moral Evolution," *ibid.*, October 9, 1878. See also G. B. Boone, "Social Evolution," *ibid.*, December 11, 1878.

96. The latter topic is covered below on pp. 75–77.

97. See the article in *Oberlin Review*, March 24, 1875.

98. See Fletcher, *A History of Oberlin College*, II, 697–700, 703–5, for early Oberlin science instruction.

99. See the manuscript lecture, "Darwin," in the A. A. Wright Papers.

100. *Oberlin Review*, June 9, 1875.

101. Albert A. Wright to Mrs. Albert A. Wright, October 4, 1876, A. A. Wright Papers. For a historical account of the teaching of botany at Oberlin, see the article by William P. Holt in the *Oberlin Review*, March 9, 1898.

102. *Ibid.*, September 11, 1878, September 25, 1878. See also Frank F. and Francis Jewett, "The Chemical Department of Oberlin College from 1833 to 1912," *Oberlin Alumni Magazine*, XVIII, No. 10, Supplement (July, 1922), 3-15.

103. *Oberlin News*, September 27, 1878.

104. *Annual Report of the President for 1879*, p. 3.

105. Gladys Bryson, "The Emergence of the Social Sciences from Moral Philosophy," *International Journal of Ethics*, XLII, No. 3 (April, 1932), 304-23; "The Comparable Interests of the Old Moral Philosophy and the Modern Social Sciences," *Social Forces*, XI, No. 1 (October, 1932), 19-27; "Sociology Considered as Moral Philosophy," *Sociological Review*, XXIV, No. 1 (January, 1932), 26-36; Anna Haddow, *Political Science in American Colleges and Universities, 1636-1900* (New York: D. Appleton-Century Co., 1939), pp. 171-234; Michael J. L. O'Connor, *Origins of Academic Economics in the United States* (New York: Columbia University Press, 1944.

106. For the content of Fairchild's course in Moral Philosophy, see his textbook *Moral Science or the Philosophy of Obligation* (New York: American Book Co., 1892). The first edition was published in 1869 with the title *Moral Philosophy or the Science of Obligation*.

107. For Walker's appointment and his teaching, see Fletcher, *A History of Oberlin College*, II, 706–8. For an exposition of his economic ideas, see Joseph Dorfman, *The Economic Mind in American Civilization* (5 vols.; New York: Viking Press, 1946-59), II, 749-52, III, 49-56.

108. See Fletcher, *A History of Oberlin College*, II, 708; *Oberlin Review*, October 9, 1878; April 3, 1878; January 22, 1879; February 5, 1879; March 3, 1883; May 12, 1883.

109. A biographical sketch of Monroe by James H. Fairchild is in the *Oberlin Review*, June 24, 1896. See also Fletcher, *A History of Oberlin College*, I, 390.

110. *Annual Report of the President for 1880*, p. 8.

111. Jacob Dolson Cox to James Monroe, July 5, 1881, Henry Cowles to James Monroe, July 8, 1881, Monroe Papers.

112. Trustees' Minutes, June 26, 1882, June 29, 1883; *Annual Report of the President for 1882*, p. 13.

113. James Monroe to James H. Fairchild, January 1, 1886, Monroe Papers.

114. In an interesting letter to Monroe, Andrew D. White described the methods used in teaching history at Cornell University. Monroe followed White's advice only in part. Andrew D. White to James Monroe, December 31, 1884, Monroe Papers. See also Etta Wright, "Notes on Professor James Monroe's Courses, Modern History and Political Economy, 1891," (Oberlin College Library); Robert Samuel Fletcher, "History in Oberlin," *Oberlin Alumni Magazine*, XLVIII, No. 1 (November, 1951), 4, 15.

115. For student appreciation of Monroe's teaching, see the *Oberlin Review*, April 26, 1887; September 26, 1894; February 20, 1895; Alfred D. Sheffield to Robert S. Fletcher, August 8, 1949 (loaned to the author by Mrs. Robert S. Fletcher).

116. Thomas Nixon Carver, *Recollections of an Unplanned Life* (Los Angeles: Ward Ritchie Press, 1949), p. 120.

117. Charles B. Martin stated that these Thursday Lectures of Monroe's were the best of their time. Martin, p. 21.

118. Notes and lectures on political economy, Monroe Papers; John T. Ellis, "Notes on Professor James Monroe's Course, Advanced Political Economy, 1894," (Oberlin College Library).

119. *Oberlin Review*, September 27, 1887. There is a great deal of material on the seminar in the Monroe Papers.

120. Faculty Minutes, December 10, 1894.

121. Henry F. May, *Protestant Churches and Industrial America* (New York: Harper and Bros., 1949), pp. 39-87.

122. *Oberlin Review*, May 29, 1878.

123. *Ibid.*, December 25, 1879.

124. See May, pp. 91-111, and Charles H. Hopkins, *The Rise of the Social Gospel in American Protestantism, 1865-1915* ("Yale Studies in Religious Education," Vol. XIV; New Haven: Yale University Press, 1940), pp. 3-49, for discussions of the breakdown of complacency in some Protestant groups.

125. *Oberlin Review*, September 23, 1883.

126. A probable source of these ideas was the Reverend Josiah Strong's book *Our Country: Its Possible Future and its Present Crisis* (New York, Baker and Taylor, 1885), published under the auspices of the Congregationalist Home Missionary Society. Strong, a leading Ohio Congregationalist and a member of the Oberlin Board of Trustees from 1881 to 1887, preached and delivered public addresses at the College on several occasions during those years.

127. "A Plea for Restricted Immigration," *Oberlin Review*, April 26, 1887.

128. *Ibid.*

129. *Ibid.*

130. *Ibid.*, February 6, 1886.

131. See Sidney E. Mead, "American Protestantism since the Civil War. I. From Denominationalism to Americanism," *Journal of Religion*, XXXVI, No. 1 (January, 1956), 1-16.

132. *Oberlin Review,* June 25, 1889.

133. As only a few of many examples, see the orations and essays in *ibid.,* February 17, 1883; March 3, 1883; December 7, 1886; May 1, 1888; June 22, 1892; May 5, 1897; January 19, 1899.

134. *Ibid.,* December 18, 1880; January 10, 1894; November 18, 1896; May 25, 1898; February 2, 1899.

135. *Ibid.,* February 19, 1879.

136. *Ibid.*

137. *Ibid.*

138. *Ibid.*

139. "The Church an Aristocracy," *ibid.,* June 29, 1886.

140. *Ibid.,* July 19, 1876; June 3, 1890.

141. "Third-Class Humanity," *ibid.,* May 14, 1879.

142. "Regnant Americanism," *ibid.,* May 8, 1895.

143. *Ibid.,* April 17, 1886.

144. *Ibid.,* November 6, 1888.

145. *Ibid.,* February 19, 1889.

146. Settlement house work was discussed in many articles and orations. See *ibid.,* January 26, 1892; May 31, 1892; November 7, 1894; May 15, 1895; November 27, 1895; March 4, 1896.

147. Eloise Steele, "College Settlements," *ibid.,* March 4, 1896.

148. See Hartson, *Vocational Guidance Magazine,* VI, No. 7, 300-302, for alumni career statistics in social settlements and other branches of social work.

149. Clarissa R. Commons to James H. Fairchild, March 24, 1881, Fairchild Papers; John R. Commons, *Myself* (New York: Macmillan Co., 1934), pp. 7-38; "Journal of Professor Lyman B. Hall," I, 107, 147; *Oberlin Review,* January 24, 1888; Robert Samuel Fletcher, "An Oberlin Liberal," *Oberlin Alumni Magazine,* XLVI, No. 4 (April, 1950), 13-14.

150. *Oberlin Review,* May 15, 1888.

151. *Ibid.,* February 7, 1888.

152. All quotations from *ibid.*

153. Commons, *Myself,* p. 38.

154. See, for example, the *Oberlin Review,* December 19, 1885.

155. *Ibid.,* March 29, 1887. See also Mary B. Shurtleff to Giles W. Shurtleff, March 24, 1887, Shurtleff Papers.

156. *Oberlin Review,* November 22, 1887; June 28, 1887.

157. The Constitution and minutes of the Club are in the Oberlin College Library. The quotations are from that manuscript. See also *Oberlin Review,* January 7, 1888; February 24, 1888.

158. Fletcher, *Oberlin Alumni Magazine,* XLVI, No. 4, 13.

159. Commons, *Myself,* p. 38.

160. *Oberlin Review,* April 30, 1890; January 21, 1891.

161. James Monroe, "The Theories of Mr. Henry George as found in 'Progress and Poverty,'" Monroe Papers.

162. *Oberlin Review,* May 26, 1891.

163. The only Oberlin student known to the author to have been associated with a utopian experiment was Ralph Albertson, who attended the seminary in 1888-1889 and in 1890-1891 and later became one of the leaders of the Christian

Commonwealth Colony in Georgia. James Dombrowski, *The Early Days of Christian Socialism in America* (New York: Columbia University Press, 1936), pp. 132-70.

164. *Oberlin Review*, February 7, 1887.

165. See Fairchild's baccalaureate sermon of 1886 printed in Swing, pp. 302-22, under the title "The Golden Rule and the Labor Question."

166. Fairchild, *Moral Science*, p. 248.

167. *Oberlin Review*, July 8, 1874.

168. Martin, p. 26.

169. *Oberlin Review*, January 22, 1879.

170. *Annual Report of the President for 1888*, pp. 6-7.

171. *Annual Report of the President for 1887*, p. 5.

172. Charles B. Martin to Lyman B. Hall, June 30, 1885, Hall Papers, describing conversations with several New York City alumni.

173. Merritt Starr to James Monroe, June 23, 1887, Norman P. Willard to James Monroe, June 23, 1887, Monroe Papers.

174. "Journal of Professor Lyman B. Hall," I, 125.

175. A copy of the original prospectus, dated March 30, 1887, is in the Monroe Papers.

176. "Journal of Professor Lyman B. Hall," I, 126.

177. *Ibid.*, I, 128.

178. See the account in the *Oberlin Review*, October 25, 1887.

179. Merritt Starr to James H. Fairchild, June 8, 1887; Norman P. Willard to James H. Fairchild, July 13, 1887, Fairchild Papers; C. C. Creegan to Giles W. Shurtleff, June 29, 1887, Shurtleff Papers.

180. *Oberlin Review*, October 25, 1887; "Journal of Professor Lyman B. Hall," I, 128-29. For a discussion of some points raised, see the *Oberlin Review*, December 20, 1887; January 10, 1888; January 24, 1888; February 7, 1888.

181. *Ibid.*, April 29, 1874.

182. For discussion of this, see *ibid.*, March 10, 1875; February 23, 1876; May 1, 1888; February 19, 1889. The last citation gives percentages of graduates entering the ministry from Oberlin and from other colleges.

183. Editorial by John R. Commons, *ibid.*, June 26, 1888. For a similar statement, see the editorial by H. A. Weld on "Original Class Work," *ibid.*, January 10, 1888.

CHAPTER III

1. For Fairchild's hope that Ellis would be chosen, see Swing, pp. 323–24. Hundreds of letters in the Fairchild Papers, and many in the Monroe Papers, G. F. Wright Papers, and Hall Papers, bear on the choice of a president, most of them revealing a measure of anxiety.

2. Samuel F. Cooper to James H. Fairchild, May 14, 1889, Fairchild Papers.

3. Charles C. Creegan to James H. Fairchild, May 15, 1889, Fairchild Papers.

4. The final faculty statement, submitted to the board on January 22, 1890, showed that sixteen favored the election of King and seven favored Ellis. Trustees'

Minutes, January 22, 1890; "Journal of Professor Lyman B. Hall," I, 206. See also A. S. Root to L. B. Hall, April 5, 1889, Hall Papers; P. C. Hayes to James Monroe, June 10, 1889, Monroe Papers; Martin, "Reminiscences of Charles B. Martin," p. 16.

5. "Journal of Professor Lyman B. Hall," I, 205; Trustees' Minutes, March 5, 1890; Albert B. Nettleton to James H. Fairchild, May 19, 1890, Samuel J. Cooper to James H. Fairchild, June 16, 1890, Fairchild Papers.

6. Trustees' Minutes, June 30, 1890; "Journal of Professor Lyman B. Hall," I, 216, 218; four letters of Lucy Kenaston (President Fairchild's daughter) to Carl A. Kenaston, June 30, 1890; July 6, 1890; July 11, 1890; July 18, 1890, Fairchild Papers; Merrill Gates to George F. Wright, July 18, 1890, G. F. Wright Papers; Henry M. Tenney to members of the board of trustees, August 7, 1890, Monroe Papers; L. C. Warner to James H. Fairchild, August 21, 1890, Fairchild Papers.

7. See the exchange of letters between Rev. Dan F. Bradley, Merritt Starr, and N. W. Bates in the *Oberlin Review*, October 21, 1890; November 4, 1890; November 11, 1890; November 18, 1890.

8. A recent account is in George E. Peterson, *The New England College in the Age of the University* (Amherst, Mass.: Amherst College Press, 1964), pp. 126–36. See also Claude M. Fuess, *Amherst, the Story of a New England College* (Boston: Little, Brown & Co., 1935), pp. 246–57, and Thomas LeDuc, *Piety and Intellect at Amherst College, 1865–1912* ("Columbia Studies in American Culture," No. 16; New York: Columbia University Press, 1946), pp. 136–37.

9. Trustees' Minutes, January 28, 1891; "Journal of Professor Lyman B. Hall," II, 2–3.

10. "Journal of Professor Lyman B. Hall," II, 3. See also the account of the celebrations in the *Oberlin Review*, February 3, 1891.

11. See Martin, "Reminiscences of Charles B. Martin," p. 16, and the *Oberlin Review*, February 3, 1891, for biographical information.

12. *Addresses on the Occasion of the Inauguration of William G. Ballantine as President of Oberlin College*. Ballantine's address, entitled "The American College," is on pp. 9–19.

13. For a similar, later statement, see the account of a Thursday lecture by Ballantine in the *Oberlin Review*, November 22, 1893.

14. *Addresses on the Occasion of the Inauguration of William G. Ballantine as President of Oberlin College*, pp. 14, 18–19.

15. *Ibid.*, pp. 12–15.

16. *Ibid.*, 20–44.

17. *Ibid.*, pp. 21–22.

18. *Ibid.*, p. 22.

19. Address of Mrs. Martha C. Kincaid, representative of the College alumnae, in *ibid.*, pp. 26–27.

20. *Ibid.*, pp. 33–34.

21. *Ibid.*, p. 35.

22. *Ibid.*, p. 38.

23. *Ibid.*

24. *Ibid.*

25. *Ibid.*, pp. 37–38.

26. *Ibid.*, p. 39.

27. For an elaboration of some of these points, see King's address, "Personal and Ideal Elements in Education," delivered as a Thursday lecture on November 3, 1892, in the *Oberlin Review*, November 9, 1892.

28. For King's career until 1902, the year of his election to the presidency of Oberlin, see Love, pp. 1–93.

29. Henry Churchill King, *Reconstruction in Theology* (New York: The Macmillan Co., 1901).

30. Henry Churchill King, *Theology and the Social Consciousness: A Study of the Relations of the Social Consciousness to Theology* (New York: The Macmillan Co., 1902).

31. For a bibliography of King's more important writings, see Love, pp. 288–91.

32. King, *Reconstruction in Theology*, p. 3.

33. *Ibid.*, p. 49.

34. Walter M. Horton, "Henry Churchill King and Oberlin Liberalism," *Oberlin Today*, XVIII, No. 3 (Third Quarter, 1960), 9–11.

35. King, *Reconstruction in Theology*, pp. 61–80, 88–91.

36. *Catalogue of Oberlin College, 1890–1891*, p. 56; Horton, *Oberlin Today*, XVIII, No. 3, p. 7.

37. For information on the resignation, see Thomas N. Carver to Robert S. Fletcher, January 25, 1949 (loaned to the author by Mrs. Robert S. Fletcher); "Journal of Professor Lyman B. Hall," III, 39; Carver, p. 129; Love, p. 64; Keeler, p. 177.

38. Trustees' Minutes, October 12, 1896.

39. Trustees' Minutes, November 29, 1898; *Oberlin Review*, December 8, 1898.

40. For a sketch of Barrows' life, see the article by Shailer Mathews in the *Dictionary of American Biography*. Initial reactions of Oberlin professors are recorded in the "Journal of Professor Lyman B. Hall," III, 189 ff.; two letters of Albert A. Wright to Helen B. Wright, January 18, 1899, February 26, 1899, A. A. Wright Papers; Martin, "Reminiscences of Charles B. Martin," p. 17.

41. The address is printed in the *Oberlin Review*, June 21, 1899.

42. *Annual Reports of the President and Treasurer of Oberlin College for 1900*, p. 18. See also some remarks of Professor Albert H. Currier, printed in the *Oberlin Review*, June 12, 1902.

43. The table includes only those whose major duty was teaching college students. The information was drawn principally from *Oberlin College, Alumni Register*, Int. 21–56.

44. The following persons composed the college faculty in 1891–92: Frederick Anderegg, associate professor of mathematics; Edward I. Bosworth, professor of English Bible; William B. Chamberlain, professor of elocution and rhetoric; Charles H. Churchill, professor of physics and astronomy; John R. Commons, associate professor of political economy; Mrs. Abbie F. Eaton, instructor in German; John M. Ellis, professor of mental and moral philosophy; William G. Frost, professor of Greek; Lyman B. Hall, professor of Latin; Charles Harris, professor of German; Frank F. Jewett, professor of chemistry; Mrs. Adelia A. F. Johnston, professor of medieval history; Henry C. King, professor of philosophy; Charles B. Martin, assistant professor of Latin and Greek; James Monroe, professor of political science and modern history; Harry H. Powers, professor of French; William I. Thomas, professor of English; Worrallo Whitney, instructor in botany; Albert A. Wright, professor of geology and natural history.

45. The members of the faculty in 1901–2 were: Arletta M. Abbott, professor of German; Frederick Anderegg, professor of mathematics; Mary E. Barrows, instructor in English composition; E. L. Bogart, associate professor of political economy and sociology; William D. Cairns, instructor in mathematics; Kirke L. Cowdery, instructor in French; Walter Dennison, professor of Latin; Frederick O. Grover, professor of botany; Lyman B. Hall, professor of history; Frank F. Jewett, professor of chemistry; Lynds Jones, instructor in zoology; Henry C. King, pro-

fessor of theology and philosophy; Fred E. Leonard, professor of physiology; Alice H. Luce, professor of English; Simon F. MacLennan, professor of psychology and pedagogy; Charles B. Martin, professor of Greek literature and archaeology; Charles E. St. John, professor of physics and astronomy; Charles H. A. Wager, professor of English; John R. Wightman, professor of Romance languages and literature; Albert A. Wright, professor of geology and zoology.

46. See Martin, "Reminiscences of Charles B. Martin," p. 48.

47. Trustees' Minutes, March 4–5, 1896.

48. "Journal of Professor Lyman B. Hall," III, 139, 141.

49. Ibid., pp. 143, 146–47, 193–99; Trustees' Minutes, June 20, 1898, March 8, 1899.

50. Carver, p. 113.

51. E. L. Bogart to Robert S. Fletcher, January 9, 1953 (loaned to the author by Mrs. Robert S. Fletcher).

52. Millikan, p. 57.

53. Martin, "Reminiscences of Charles B. Martin," pp. 16, 48; Annual Report of the President for 1892, pp. 3–4.

54. Annual Report of the President for 1898, p. 5.

55. Commons, p. 49.

56. William G. Ballantine to James H. Fairchild, March 22, 1893, Fairchild Papers; William G. Ballantine to Lyman B. Hall, April 21, 1894, Hall Papers.

57. See the Catalogue of Oberlin College, 1890–1891, pp. 3–4; Annual Report of the President for 1891, p. 4; Annual Report of the President for 1895, p. 6. For a comparison of Oberlin admissions standards with those of nineteen other colleges, see the Oberlin Review, October 10, 1894.

58. Annual Reports of the President and Treasurer of Oberlin College for 1900, p. 46; "Journal of Professor Lyman B. Hall," IV, 25; Faculty Minutes, February 11, 1901.

59. Catalogue of Oberlin College, 1900–1901, p. 77; Annual Reports of the President and Treasurer of Oberlin College for 1900, p. 47.

60. Annual Report of the President for 1891, p. 4.

61. Annual Report of the President for 1892, p. 5.

62. For these changes, see the Catalogue of Oberlin College, 1900–1901, p. 77.

63. See the Oberlin Review, April 12, 1892; June 10, 1896; Annual Report of the President for 1893, p, 7.

64. Professor Lyman B. Hall, in "Report of the Department of English and American History," in the Annual Report of the President for 1898, p. 25.

65. See the Annual Report of the President for 1893, p. 20; Annual Report of the President for 1894, pp. 12, 30.

66. Annual Report of the President for 1894, p. 4.

67. Commons, pp. 40–41.

68. James Monroe to Richard T. Ely, September 29, 1888, Richard T. Ely Papers (State Historical Society of Wisconsin), cited hereafter as Ely Papers; many letters in the Monroe Papers.

69. Commons, p. 42.

70. Ibid.

71. The origin of the historical school and Ely's place in it are briefly discussed in Joseph Dorfman, The Economic Mind in American Civilization (5 vols.; New York: Viking Press, 1946–59), III, 87–92, 161–64, and more thoroughly in Jurgen Herbst, The German Historical School in American Scholarship (Ithaca, N.Y.: Cornell University Press, 1965), pp. 4, 14, 18, 44–45, 53, 134–35, 161. See also

Sidney Fine, *Laissez-Faire and the General Welfare State* (Ann Arbor Paperbacks; Ann Arbor, Mich.: University of Michigan Press, 1964), pp. 198-251.

72. There are several letters from Commons to Monroe in the Monroe Papers in which he carefully describes his work at Johns Hopkins with Ely. See especially those dated January 4, 1888 [1889]; May 14, 1889; October 25, 1889; December 19, 1889; February 27, 1890; June 7, 1890.

73. John R. Commons to James Monroe, May 14, 1889, Monroe Papers.

74. John R. Commons to James Monroe, March 16, 1891, Monroe Papers; Faculty Minutes, May 13, 1891; "Journal of Professor Lyman B. Hall," II, 10.

75. John R. Commons to James Monroe, May 11, 1891; May 18, 1891; May 25, 1891, Monroe Papers.

76. Commons, p. 47.

77. John R. Commons to Richard T. Ely, November 5, 1891, Ely Papers.

78. *Ibid.*; E. Benjamin Andrews, *Institutes of Economics* (Boston: Silver, Burdette, 1889); Richard T. Ely, *Problems of Today* (New York: Thomas Y. Crowell and Co., 1888); Richard T. Ely, *An Introduction to Political Economy* (New York: Eaton and Mains, 1889).

79. Oberlin College, *Announcement of Courses in Political Science, Sociology and History,* November, 1891; *Catalogue of Oberlin College, 1891-1892,* pp. 79-82.

80. Oberlin College, *Announcement of Courses in Political Science, Sociology and History.*

81. *Ibid.*

82. *Oberlin Review,* January 26, 1892.

83. John R. Commons, *Social Reform and the Church* (New York: Thomas Y. Crowell and Co., 1894), pp. 3-26.

84. *Ibid.,* pp. 20-21.

85. *Oberlin Review,* January 26, 1892.

86. John R. Commons, *A Popular Bibliography of Sociology* ("Oberlin College Library Bulletin," Vol. I, No. 1; Oberlin: Oberlin College Library, 1892).

87. John R. Commons to Richard T. Ely, December 24, 1891, January 13, 1892, Ely Papers; "Journal of Professor Lyman B. Hall," II, 37-38, 55; *Oberlin Review,* January 26, 1892; March 15, 1892.

88 John R. Commons to Richard T. Ely, April 28, 1892, Ely Papers; Commons, *Myself,* pp. 48-49; *Oberlin Review,* May 17, 1892.

89. *Oberlin Review,* September 20, 1892.

90. J. William Black, *Maryland's Attitude in the Struggle for Canada* ("Johns Hopkins University Studies in Historical and Political Science," 10th Series, No. 7; Baltimore: Johns Hopkins University Press, 1892).

91. The Hopkins doctorate was in history and political science. Students were required to major in one of these fields and to meet course and examination requirements in the other, with supplementary study in two related fields such as political economy and international law. For a description, see W. Stull Holt (ed.), *Historical Scholarship in the United States, 1876-1901, as Revealed in the Correspondence of Herbert B. Adams* ("Johns Hopkins University Studies in Historical and Political Science," Vol. LVI, No. 4; Baltimore: Johns Hopkins University Press, 1938), p. 15.

92. J. William Black, "Report of the Department of Political Economy," in *Annual Report of the President for 1893,* pp. 29-30; *Catalogue of Oberlin College, 1892-1893,* pp. 86-90.

93. *Oberlin Review,* September 27, 1893. The lecture was published under the title of "Savagery and Survivals," *Popular Science Monthly,* XLV (July, 1894), 388-401.

94. John T. Ellis, "Notes on Professor J. William Black's Course, Practical Sociology, Winter Term, 1893–1894," (Oberlin College Library).

95. *Ibid.*

96. Charles R. Henderson, *An Introduction to the Study of the Dependent, Defective and Delinquent Classes* (Boston: D. C. Heath and Co., 1893).

97. John T. Ellis, "Notes on Professor J. William Black's Course, Practical Sociology, Winter Term, 1893–1894."

98. J. William Black to Herbert B. Adams, March 13, 1893, in Holt, p. 194; J. William Black, "Report of the Department of Political Economy," in *Annual Report of the President for 1893*, p. 29.

99. J. William Black to Herbert B. Adams, March 13, 1893, in Holt, p. 194; *Oberlin Review*, March 8, 1893; *Oberlin News*, March 2, 1893; *Cleveland Plain Dealer*, February 28, 1893.

100. J. William Black, *References on the History of Labor and Some Contemporary Labor Problems* ("Oberlin College Library Bulletin," Vol. I, No. 2; Oberlin: Oberlin College Library, 1893).

101. *Oberlin Review*, March 7, 1894.

102. *Ibid.*

103. *Oberlin News*, March 30, 1893.

104. *Ibid.*, March 2, 1893.

105. *Oberlin Review*, May 31, 1893.

106. *Ibid.*, February 21, 1894; John T. Ellis, "Notes on Professor J. William Black's Course, Practical Sociology, Winter Term, 1893–1894"; J. William Black to Herbert B. Adams, February 19, 1894, in Holt, pp. 214–15.

107. J. William Black to Herbert B. Adams, February 19, 1894, in Holt, pp. 214–15.

108. *Ibid.; Oberlin Review*, April 11, 1894.

109. *Oberlin Review*, June 13, 1894.

110. *Ibid.*, September 26, 1894. An abridgment of his doctoral dissertation was published as "The Theory of Wages Adjusted to Recent Theories of Value," *Quarterly Journal of Economics*, VIII (July, 1894), 375–402.

111. Professor Lyman B. Hall taught the courses in history after 1895.

112. *Catalogue of Oberlin College, 1894–1895*, pp. 107–8.

113. *Oberlin Review*, September 26, 1894.

114. J. A. Hobson, *The Evolution of Modern Capitalism* (New York: Charles Scribner's Sons, 1894).

115. *Catalogue of Oberlin College, 1894–1895*, pp. 107–8, 110; *Catalogue of Oberlin College, 1895–1896*, p. 104; *Oberlin Review*, January 23, 1895.

116. *Catalogue of Oberlin College, 1895–1896*, pp. 105–6.

117. *Catalogue of Oberlin College, 1896–1897*, pp. 110–11.

118. *Catalogue of Oberlin College, 1894–1895*, pp. 107–10; *Catalogue of Oberlin College, 1895–1896*, pp. 102–6; *Catalogue of Oberlin College, 1896–1897*, pp. 110–11.

119. For remarks on his later contributions to economic theory, see Dorfman, IV and V, passim.

120. "Journal of Professor Lyman B. Hall," III, 152.

121. His distrust of reform and dislike of reformers were most clearly revealed in some public lectures he delivered at Oberlin after he had been appointed to the faculty of Harvard University. See the *Oberlin Review*, October 31, 1907, January 16, 1914; Carver, *Recollections*, p. 172.

122. *Annual Reports of the President and Treasurer of Oberlin College for* 1900, p. 85.

123. *Oberlin Review,* March 15, 1898.

124. *Ibid.,* June 9, 1883.

125. *Ibid.,* November 23, 1886; March 20, 1888; May 10, 1892; May 9, 1894; December 22, 1897; June 15, 1899.

126. *Ibid.,* March 11, 1896; Trustees' Minutes, March 4, 1896; June 22, 1896.

127. *Oberlin Review,* December 19, 1885; April 14, 1891; April 21, 1891; October 12, 1892; February 23, 1898; "Journal of Professor Lyman B. Hall," III, 129; *Oberlin News,* October 13, 1892.

128. *Oberlin Review,* June 20, 1894.

129. See George F. Wright's article "Ministers and Mobs," *Bibliotheca Sacra,* XLIX (October, 1892), 676–81; Z. Swift Holbrook to George F. Wright, October 24, 1892; February 27, 1893; March 9, 1893, G. F. Wright Papers.

130. Z. Swift Holbrook, *The Lessons of the Homestead Troubles* (Chicago; Knight, Leonard and Co., 1892).

131. "Journal of Professor Lyman B. Hall," II, 107.

132. Z. Swift Holbrook, "Christian Sociology," *Bibliotheca Sacra,* LI (October, 1894), 537–59. See also two later articles, "The American Republic and the Debs Insurrection (I)," *ibid.,* LII (January, 1895), 135–52, and "The American Republic and the Debs Insurrection (II)," *ibid.* (April, 1895), pp. 209–31. The first of these articles combined praise of unrestricted individualism with a harsh attack upon alien influences; the second condemned Debs and his role in the railroad strike of 1894 and almost all practices of unions.

133. Alfred D. Sheffield to Robert S. Fletcher, August 9, 1949 (loaned to the author by Robert S. Fletcher); *Annual Report of the President for 1894,* p. 5; *Oberlin Review,* June 13, 1894; December 19, 1894; February 6, 1895; March 13, 1895.

134. *Ibid.,* October 31, 1894.

135. *Ibid.*

136. *Oberlin News,* November 15, 1894, November 22, 1894.

137. Summaries of all the addresses were published in the *Oberlin Review,* November 21, 1894; the addresses of Gladden, Warner, and Holbrook were printed in *Bibliotheca Sacra.*

138. Program of "The Oberlin Summer School of Christian Sociology," *Oberlin Review,* March 6, 1895; March 20, 1895; April 17, 1895; May 22, 1895; *Oberlin News,* June 13, 1895.

139. *Oberlin Review,* October 2, 1895.

140. Gladden's address, entitled "The Relation of Corporations to Public Morals," was printed in *Bibliotheca Sacra,* LII (October, 1895), 607–28.

141. For summaries of the addresses see the *Oberlin Review,* October 2, 1895; *Oberlin News,* July 4, 1895.

142. William G. Ballantine to James Monroe, January 15, 1896, Monroe Papers; Stephen F. Weston to George F. Wright, March 23, 1896, G. F. Wright Papers.

143. "Record Book of the Oberlin Temperance Alliance," II, 86–87.

144. Norman H. Dohn, "The History of the Anti-Saloon League," (Doctoral dissertation, Department of History, Ohio State University), pp. 21–22.

145. From an article by W. H. Pearce on the founding of the Ohio Anti-Saloon League in the *Oberlin News,* October 22, 1903.

146. Earnest H. Cherrington, *History of the Anti-Saloon League* (Westerville, Ohio: American Issue Publishing Co., 1913, pp. 11–14.

147. "Record Book of the Oberlin Temperance Alliance," II, 21–24.

148. *Ibid.*, p. 24; *Oberlin News*, June 5, 1893.

149. *Oberlin News*, June 5, 1893.

150. *Ibid.*, June 8, 1893.

151. *Ibid.*, August 30, 1893.

152. *Ibid.*

153. "Record Book of the Oberlin Temperance Alliance," II, 28–29, 138–47; *Oberlin News*, September 7, 1893. The name first chosen was the "Ohio Anti-Liquor League," but it was soon changed to the "Ohio Anti-Saloon League."

154. Cherrington, p. 22.

155. See James H. Timberlake, *Prohibition and the Progressive Movement, 1900–1920* (Cambridge: Harvard University Press, 1963), pp. 127–31.

156. Cherrington, pp. 92–95.

157. For a sketch of Wheeler's life see the article in the *D.A.B.* by William E. Shea. A detailed account is in Justin Steuart, *Wayne Wheeler, Dry Boss* (New York: Fleming H. Revell Co., 1928). Information on his activities during the twenties may be found in Peter H. Odegard, *Pressure Politics: The Story of the Anti-Saloon League* (New York: Columbia University Press, 1928) and in Andrew Sinclair, *Prohibition: The Era of Excess* (Boston: Little, Brown & Co., 1962).

158. Quoted in Steuart, pp. 38–39.

159. Note by Louis E. Lord in *Oberlin Alumni Magazine*, II, No. 1 (October, 1905), 17.

160. *Ibid.*, No. 3 (December, 1905), 105.

161. See "Journal of Professor Lyman B. Hall," VIII, 13; IX, 386; XII, 8.

162. *Ibid.*, VIII, 232.

163. Henry C. King to A. I. Root, September 22, 1915, King Papers. Due to interlineations in this copy the wording of the original is not entirely clear.

164. As scattered examples of student support for various temperance and prohibition efforts, see the *Oberlin Review*, May 5, 1891; May 26, 1891; February 21, 1894; April 24, 1895; October 6, 1908.

165. *Annual Report of the President for 1892*, p. 6; *Annual Report of the President for 1893*, pp. 5–6.

166. *Annual Report of the President for 1892*, p. 6.

167. Harry H. Powers, "An Important Step of Progress," *Oberlin Review*, March 31, 1891.

168. *Annual Report of the President for 1891*, p. 6; *Oberlin Review*, October 20, 1891.

169. The list of courses offered and other details were reprinted in *ibid.*, January 26, 1892.

170. *Ibid.*, January 26, 1892; February 16, 1892; November 23, 1892.

171. Trustees' Minutes, June 17, 1895; March 4–5, 1896.

172. Trustees' Minutes, March 4–5, 1896.

173. *Catalogue of Oberlin College, 1896–1897*, pp. 26–27.

174. *Annual Reports of the President and Treasurer of Oberlin College for 1900*, p. 48; *Annual Report of the President for 1899*, p. 11; *Annual Report of the President for 1901*, pp. 8–9.

175. See Fairchild's "Introductory Note" to Leonard, *The Story of Oberlin*, pp. 16–17, and [Leonard], "Notes of Talks with President Fairchild, No. 1, December 20, 1894–November 16, 1897," pp. 58–59.

176. See the *Oberlin Review,* January 13, 1891; October 27, 1891; November 24, 1891; March 22, 1892; "Journal of Professor Lyman B. Hall," II, 5–6, 39, 44; *Catalogue of Oberlin College, 1895–1896,* p. 29; *Oberlin News,* March 24, 1892.

177. *Catalogue of Oberlin College, 1898–1899,* pp. 30–31.

178. *Catalogue of Oberlin College, 1900–1901,* p. 43.

179. For discussions of this, see the *Oberlin Review,* November 13, 1895; November 4, 1896; January 19, 1898; October 27, 1898.

180. *Ibid.,* April 1, 1890.

181. The article is entitled, "The Day of Prayer for Colleges; a Word to the Individual Student," *ibid.,* January 29, 1896.

182. See *ibid.,* November 24, 1891; Carver, *Recollections,* p. 118.

183. On Mills' preaching and ideas, see William G. McLoughlin, *Modern Revivalism: Charles Grandison Finney to Billy Graham* (New York: Ronald Press, 1959), pp. 329–42.

184. "Journal of Professor Lyman B. Hall," I, 223–24.

185. *Oberlin Review,* October 7, 1890; October 28, 1890. See also Martin, "Reminiscences of Charles B. Martin," p. 32; "Journal of Professor Lyman B. Hall," I, 223–25, 227.

186. *Report of the President of the Trustees for 1890,* p. 5.

187. *Oberlin Review,* January 30, 1895; February 6, 1895.

188. See Ballantine's *Annual Report of the President for 1894,* p. 4.

189. For President Henry C. King's considered view of the relative merits of Christian training and a very restrained revivalism, see his essay, "Christian Training and the Revival as Methods of Converting Men: A Historical and Psychological Study," in *Personal and Ideal Elements in Education* (New York: Macmillan Co., 1904), pp. 129–235.

190. See the editorials in the *Oberlin Review,* January 17, 1894; October 17, 1894; November 7, 1894; November 17, 1898; February 16, 1899.

191. See, for example, *ibid.,* October 19, 1892; October 26, 1892; November 2, 1892, for an exchange between students and faculty on the ten o'clock rule in which President Ballantine defended it on the ground that it helped to create a homelike atmosphere.

192. See *ibid.,* October 20, 1898; *Annual Report of the President for 1898,* p. 15; *Annual Reports of the President and Treasurer of Oberlin College for 1900,* pp. 26–29; "Journal of Professor Lyman B. Hall," III, 174–76.

193. Pamphlet by Henry C. King, *Some Changes in the Regulations Governing College Students.*

194. Albert A. Wright to Helen B. Wright, March 13, 1899, A. A. Wright Papers; W. W. Cressy, "Report of the Dean of the College Department," in the *Annual Report of the President for 1898,* p. 15.

195. "Journal of Professor Lyman B. Hall," III, 175–76; Albert A. Wright to Helen B. Wright, March 13, 1899, A. A. Wright Papers; Anna Baker to Lyman B. Hall, June 15, 1900, Hall Papers.

196. *Oberlin Review,* March 23, 1899.

197. Edward I. Bosworth to Lyman B. Hall, March 24, 1894; William G. Ballantine to Lyman B. Hall, March 29, 1894; Giles W. Shurtleff to Lyman B. Hall, April 5, 1894, Hall Papers.

198. Charles C. Creegan to James H. Fairchild, June 23, 1893, Fairchild Papers. See also student editorials and articles in the *Oberlin Review,* October 20, 1891; November 22, 1893.

199. John A. R. Rogers to James H. Fairchild, April 17, 1895, Fairchild Papers.

200. For typical student statements on the need for more rigorous intellectual training, see the *Oberlin Review*, March 8, 1893; November 1, 1893; May 2, 1894; October 24, 1894; November 6, 1896.

201. F. N. Spindler, "Scholarly Enthusiasm," *ibid.*, March 7, 1894.

202. *Ibid.*

203. For one example, see *ibid.*, May 22, 1895.

204. His article is in *ibid.*, April 10, 1895. At the time Durand was a graduate student at Cornell University. He was a member of the Oberlin board of trustees from 1911 until 1952.

205. *Ibid.*

206. *Ibid.*

### CHAPTER IV

1. Florence Fitch to her parents, March 13, 1904, Florence Fitch Papers (Oberlin College Library). Cited hereafter as Fitch Papers.

2. Trustees' Minutes, November 19, 1902; "Journal of Professor Lyman B. Hall," IV, 186. See also Donald M. Love, *Henry Churchill King of Oberlin* (New Haven: Yale University Press, 1956), p. 103.

3. For student opinion in 1902, see the letters of John G. Olmstead to his parents, November 20, 1902; November 21, 1902, John G. Olmstead Papers (Oberlin College Library). Cited hereafter as Olmstead Papers.

4. See Love, pp. 224-49, for the postwar period at Oberlin and for King's lack of close contact with currents of student life.

5. Information on the board has been taken from *Oberlin College, Alumni Register*, Int. 21-57.

6. These and the following figures were compiled from *ibid.*, Int. 21-56.

7. Henry C. King to Rev. Frank N. White, February 20, 1907, King Papers.

8. "Journal of Professor Lyman B. Hall," VIII, 71.

9. Interview with A. B. Wolfe, professor of economics and sociology, 1905-14, February 20, 1960; Henry C. King to James A. Blaisdell, May 10, 1916, King Papers; "Journal of Professor Lyman B. Hall," XI, 232; Love, pp. 151-52.

10. See the *Catalogue of Oberlin College, 1910-1911*, pp. 116-19; *Oberlin Alumni Magazine*, VII, No. 8 (May, 1911), 262-68.

11. William E. Mosher to Henry C. King, December 13, 1910, King Papers; "Journal of Professor Lyman B. Hall," IX, 143, 400; X, 67, 188.

12. *Catalogue of Oberlin College, 1913-1914*, p. 121; Love, pp. 130-63.

13. *Oberlin Review*, March 22, 1911.

14. *Ibid.*, April 12, 1911.

15. John G. Olmstead, "Oberlin Spirit," Olmstead Papers. There are many similar evaluations in student writings. See, for example, Dahl B. Cooper to Henry C. King, December 7, 1903; December 17, 1906, King Papers; *Oberlin Review*, April 30, 1908.

16. Olmstead, "Oberlin Spirit." Some charged that a color line existed at Oberlin in the early twentieth century. Though segregation was contrary to policy and principle, and despite faculty and administrative efforts to avoid it, the evidence,

while incomplete, suggests its existence in a limited way. See the *Oberlin Alumni Magazine*, VI, No. 6 (March, 1910), 224; VI, No. 7 (April, 1910), 250–51.

17. Comments in margin of Olmstead, "Oberlin Spirit."

18. King, *Reconstruction in Theology*, p. 169.

19. *Ibid.*

20. *Ibid.*, pp. 169–71.

21. *Ibid.*, pp. 190–91.

22. *Ibid.*, pp. 199–200.

23. *Ibid.*, p. 223.

24. *Ibid.*, p. 225.

25. *Ibid.*, p. 211.

26. See Frank H. Foster, *The Modern Movement in American Theology* (New York: Fleming H. Revell Co., 1939), pp. 186–87.

27. King, *Theology and Social Consciousness*, pp. 111–12, quoting Francis G. Peabody, *Jesus Christ and the Social Question* (New York: The Macmillan Co., 1900), p. 104.

28. *Addresses on the Occasion of the Inauguration of William G. Ballantine as President of Oberlin College*, p. 38.

29. For parallel developments in the national Y.M.C.A. organization, see Hopkins, *Rise of the Social Gospel*, pp. 298–300; Hopkins, *History of the Y.M.C.A.*, pp. 510–38.

30. See the *Oberlin Review*, March 12, 1903; April 28, 1904; June 1, 1905; May 24, 1906.

31. *Ibid.*, November 19, 1903.

32. *Ibid.*, April 28, 1904.

33. *Ibid.*, October 20, 1904; February 21, 1907; February 15, 1910.

34. *Ibid.*, October 31, 1911.

35. See *ibid.*, September 28, 1910; Jeremiah W. Jenks, *The Political and Social Significance of the Life and Teachings of Jesus* (New York: Young Men's Christian Association Press, 1906).

36. *Ibid.*, p. vii.

37. John G. Olmstead to Louise Hutchinson, October 15, 1908, Olmstead Papers.

38. See King's article "The Day of Prayer for Colleges: A Word to the Individual Student," in the *Oberlin Review*, January 30, 1902.

39. "Journal of Professor Lyman B. Hall," V, 6–7.

40. John G. Olmstead to his parents, February 2, 1903, Olmstead Papers. For an account of the meeting, see the *Oberlin Review*, February 5, 1903.

41. "Journal of Professor Kemper Fullerton," January 26, 1905. See also the *Oberlin Review*, February 2, 1905.

42. *Oberlin Review*, January 19, 1905.

43. *Ibid.*, February 8, 1906. For a lengthy lament by a former professor over the spiritual decline at Oberlin, see the interesting letters from William G. Frost to Henry C. King, October 1, 1907; October 13, 1907, and Ellen Frost to King, n.d. and the reply of King to Frost, October 7, 1907, King Papers.

44. *Ibid.*, November 25, 1913.

45. *Ibid.*, February 2, 1909.

46. *Program for the Week of Prayer* (Oberlin College Library), See also the *Oberlin Review*, February 4, 1916; February 15, 1916; February 22, 1916; March 3, 1916; March 7, 1916; *Annual Report of the President for 1915–1916*, p. 136.

47. *Oberlin Alumni Magazine*, XII, No. 7 (April, 1916), 181.

48. "President King's Training Class for Christian Workers," Miscellaneous Material (Oberlin College Library); *Oberlin Alumni Magazine*, IV, No. 2 (November, 1907), 50–51.

49. See "Journal of Professor Lyman B. Hall," VII, 109, and King's explanatory statement in the *Oberlin Alumni Magazine*, III, No. 2 (November, 1906), 66–67.

50. "Journal of Professor Lyman B. Hall," IX, 378, 387; XI, 86, 270.

51. Professor Karl W. Gehrkens to Henry C. King, December 20, 1915, King Papers.

52. Henry C. King to C. C. North, March 3, 1904; Henry C. King to Mrs. Henry Clay Worth, September 22, 1905, King Papers; *Oberlin Review*, March 2, 1905.

53. "Journal of Professor Lyman B. Hall," X, 164, 175.

54. *Catalogue of Oberlin College, 1912–1913*, p. 126.

55. "Journal of Professor Lyman B. Hall," X, 101; XI, 6.

56. *Oberlin Review*, November 26, 1903; October 18, 1906; December 13, 1906; April 27, 1909; January 19, 1910; March 2, 1910; May 26, 1911; February 27, 1912; December 6, 1912; January 24, 1913; November 7, 1913; April 14, 1914; Walter Rauschenbusch to Henry C. King, September 21, 1909, King Papers; "Journal of Professor Lyman B. Hall," VII, 118; IX, 153; X, 245; XII, 55; "Journal of Professor Kemper Fullerton," October 11, 1906; *Annual Report of the President for 1913–1914*, p. 86; *Oberlin Alumni Magazine*, VI, No. 3 (December, 1909), 105–6; VI, No. 5 (February, 1910), 188–89; IX, No. 4 (January, 1913), 140–41; XI, No. 1 (October, 1914), 5–6.

57. *Oberlin Review*, February 9, 1905; November 16, 1905; January 14, 1913.

58. *Ibid.*, October 8, 1912; October 15, 1912; "Journal of Professor Lyman B. Hall," X, 132.

59. Statement of Hamilton Holt quoted in the *Oberlin Review*, April 19, 1912; Walter Rauschenbusch to Henry C. King, July 2, 1912; Charles M. Sheldon to Henry C. King, February 4, 1914; Josiah Strong to Henry C. King, February 18, 1915, King Papers.

60. Quoted in the *Oberlin Review*, May 17, 1912. A slightly different wording is given in the *Oberlin News*, May 15, 1912.

61. *Oberlin Review*, May 24, 1912.

62. Albert B. Wolfe, "Social Focus of College Studies: To What Extent Do the Subjects Pursued during the Four Years of the College Course Show a Tendency toward a Social Focus? An Investigation of the Programs of Students in One College," *Religious Education*, IX (April, 1914), 141–54. See the tributes in the *Oberlin Alumni Magazine*, XXI, No. 10 (July, 1925), 26–27; Herbert A. Miller to Henry C. King, December 8, 1915, King Papers; Mildred Newman and Martha Belknap, "The Relation of Sociology to Social Service among Oberlin Graduates" (Oberlin College Library), p. 14.

63. Quoted in *Annual Report of the President for 1906–1907*, p. 171.

64. Quoted in *Annual Report of the President for 1908–1909*, p. 255.

65. *Oberlin Review*, May 10, 1906; February 18, 1907; February 27, 1908; April 9, 1912.

66. *Ibid.*, March 5, 1912.

67. *Ibid.*, April 16, 1903; April 14, 1904; May 12, 1904; November 3, 1904; March 2, 1905; March 9, 1905; March 7, 1907; March 21, 1907; April 23, 1908; March 8, 1911; December 13, 1912; April 21, 1913.

68. *Ibid.*, March 16, 21; April 18; May 16, 23; October 3, 31; November 21, 28, 1907; February 23; March 5, 12, 19, 22; April 5, 9, 16, 23; May 3, 17, 24, 1912.

69. *Ibid.*, October 17; November 3, 14, 28, 1911.

70. *Ibid.*, March 12, 1915.

71. *Ibid.*, November 23, 1915; December 7, 14, 21, 1915; January 18, February 29, March 3, 10, 1916; "Journal of Professor Lyman B. Hall," XI, 240.

72. A file of the *Rational Patriot* is in the Oberlin College Library. See also the *Oberlin Alumni Magazine*, XVIII, No. 4 (January, 1922), 27, and XVIII, No. 5 (February, 1922), 19.

73. *Oberlin Review*, May 9, 1916.

74. Henry Churchill King, *The Moral and Religious Challenge of Our Times* (New York: The Macmillan Co., 1911).

75. Hopkins, *Rise of the Social Gospel*, p. 215.

76. King, *Moral and Religious Challenge of Our Times*, p. 75.

77. *Ibid.*, pp. 75–76.

78. *Ibid.*, p. 76.

79. *Ibid.*, pp. 316–42.

80. *Ibid.*, p. 326.

81. *Ibid.*, p. 330.

82. *Ibid.*, p. 334.

83. *Ibid.*, p. 339.

84. *Ibid.*, p. 341.

85. *Ibid.*, pp. 341–42.

86. *Ibid.*, p. 74.

# BIBLIOGRAPHY

PRIMARY SOURCES

## Manuscript Materials

Unless otherwise noted, the following manuscripts are located in the Oberlin College Library.

### Collections of Papers

Castle, Henry Northrup. University of Chicago Library.
Ely, Richard T. State Historical Society of Wisconsin.
Fairchild, James Harris.
Fitch, Florence.
Hall, Lyman Bronson.
King, Henry Churchill.
Monroe, James.
Newton, Abel. State Historical Society of Wisconsin.
Olmstead, John Griffith.
Shurtleff, Giles Waldo.
Wright, Albert Allen.
Wright, George Frederick.

### Miscellaneous Manuscript Materials

ELLIS, JOHN T. "Notes on Professor James Monroe's Course, Advanced Political Economy, 1894."
———. "Notes on Professor J. William Black's Course, Practical Sociology, Winter Term, 1893–1894."
FULLERTON, KEMPER, "Journal of Professor Kemper Fullerton."
GOLDSBURY, MAY L. "Diary."
HALL, LYMAN BRONSON. "Journal of Professor Lyman B. Hall."
Henry George Club. Constitution and Minutes.
[LEONARD, DELAVAN L.]. "Notes of Talks with President Fairchild, December 20, 1894–November 16, 1897." Nos. 1–2.
MARTIN, CHARLES BEEBE. "Reminiscences of Charles B. Martin."
METCALF, ANNA M. "Notes on Professor John M. Ellis' Course, Evidences of Christianity, Spring 1882.

NEWMAN, MILDRED and MARTHA BELKNAP. "The Relation of Sociology to Social Service among Oberlin Graduates."

Oberlin College. Minutes of the Board of Trustees. Secretary's Office. Oberlin College.

———. Faculty Minutes. Secretary's Office. Oberlin College.

Oberlin Temperance Alliance. Record Book. 2 vols.

SHAW, ARCHER H. "Charles Henry Churchill."

WRIGHT, ETTA. "Notes on Professor James Monroe's Courses, Modern History and Political Economy, 1891."

## Autobiography

### Books

CARVER, THOMAS NIXON. Recollections of an Unplanned Life. Los Angeles: The Ward Ritchie Press, 1949.

COMMONS, JOHN ROGERS. Myself. New York: Macmillan Co., 1934.

EGGLESTON, MARGARET W. (ed.). Kathie's Diary. New York: George H. Doran Co., 1926.

FROST, WILLIAM G. For the Mountains, An Autobiography. New York: Fleming H. Revell Co., 1939.

MILLIKAN, ROBERT A. The Autobiography of Robert A. Millikan. New York: Prentice-Hall, Inc., 1950.

SNIDER, DENTON JACQUES. A Writer of Books in His Genesis. St. Louis: Sigma Publishing Co., n. d.

TERRELL, MARY CHURCH. A Colored Woman in a White World. Washington: Ransdell, Inc., 1940.

WARNER, LUCIEN CALVIN, Personal Memoirs of L. C. Warner. New York: Association Press, 1915.

WHITNEY, FRANK PECK. School and I: The Autobiography of an Ohio Schoolmaster. Yellow Springs, Ohio: The Antioch Press, 1957.

WRIGHT, GEORGE FREDERICK. Story of My Life and Work. Oberlin, Ohio: Bibliotheca Sacra Co., 1916.

### Articles

BRADLEY, DAN. F. "Between Classes," Oberlin Alumni Magazine, XXIX, No. 10 (July, 1933), 297–300.

———. "Then and Now," Oberlin Alumni Magazine, XXVIII, No. 3 (December, 1931), 71–72.

BURRELL, ARTHUR T. "Oberlin Social Life in the Seventies," Oberlin Alumni Magazine, XXVIII, No. 1 (October, 1931), 8–9.

CHURCHILL, ALFRED VANCE. "Midwestern: Early Oberlin Personalities," Northwest Ohio Quarterly, XXIII, No. 4 (Autumn, 1951), 211–37.

———. "Midwestern: New England Backgrounds," Northwest Ohio Quarterly, XXIV, No. 1 (Winter, 1951–1952), 33–62.

———. "Midwestern: An Oberlin Family," Northwest Ohio Quarterly, XXVII, No. 4 (Autumn, 1955), 177–90.

———. "Midwestern: Oberlin Students, Sinners and Adolescents in the 1870s and 1880s," Northwest Ohio Quarterly, XXV, No. 1 (Winter, 1952–1953), 41–62.

———. "Midwestern: Professor Charles Henry Churchill of Oberlin," *Northwest Ohio Quarterly*, XXIV, No. 3 (Summer, 1952), 139–75.

———. "Midwestern: Scientific and Musical Beginnings at Oberlin," *Northwest Ohio Quarterly*, XXIV, No. 2 (Spring, 1952), 99–115.

———. "Midwestern: Transition at Oberlin, 1850–1887," *Northwest Ohio Quarterly*, XXIV, No. 4 (Autumn, 1952), 220–39.

JOHNSTON, ADELIA A. F. "Significant Events and Noted People," *Oberlin Alumni Magazine*, VI, No. 2 (November, 1909), 51–63.

PLACE, RUTH M. "Oberlin in Perspective," *Oberlin Alumni Magazine*, XXIX, No. 9 (June, 1933), 264–66.

WRIGHT, GEORGE FREDERICK. "The Oberlin I First Knew and Oberlin Today," *Oberlin Alumni Magazine*, XVII, No. 4 (April, 1921), 148–51.

## Newspapers

*Oberlin Review*, 1874–1917.

*Oberlin News*, 1874–1917.

## Oberlin College Publications

*Addresses on the Occasion of the Inauguration of William G. Ballantine as President of Oberlin College*, July 1, 1891.

———. *Alumni Register: Graduates and Former Students, Teaching and Administrative Staff, 1833–1960.*

———. *Announcement of Courses in the Philosophical Department, 1891–1892.*

———. *Announcement of Courses in Political Science, Sociology and History, 1891.*

———. *Announcement of Extension Lectures by Members of Oberlin College Faculty.*

———. *Annual Report of the President. 1879–1917.*

———. *Catalogue of Oberlin College. 1877–1917.*

———. *Some Changes in the Regulations Governing the College Students. 1898.*

———. *The Oberlin Summer School of Christian Sociology. 1895.*

## Writings on Oberlin and Education

### Books

BARROWS, JOHN HENRY. *The Ideals of Christian Education: The Argument for the Christian College.* Oberlin, Ohio: n. p., 1899.

ELIOT, CHARLES W. *Educational Reform: Essays and Addresses.* New York: Century Co., 1898.

FAIRCHILD, JAMES HARRIS. *Educational Arrangements and College Life at Oberlin.* New York: Edward O. Jenkins, 1866.

HOFSTADTER, RICHARD and SMITH, WILSON (eds.). *American Higher Education; A Documentary History.* 2 vols. Chicago: University of Chicago Press, 1961.

KING, HENRY CHURCHILL. *The Personal and Ideal Elements in Education.* New York: Macmillan Co., 1904.

MEAD, GEORGE, and MEAD, HELEN (eds.). *Henry Northrup Castle: Letters*. London: Privately printed, 1902.

SHUMWAY, A. L., and BROWN, C. DeW. *Oberliniana: A Jubilee Volume of Semi-Historical Anecdotes Connected with the Past and Present of Oberlin College*. Cleveland: Home Publishing Co., 1883.

### Articles

MABIE, HAMILTON W. "The Intellectual Movement in the West," *Atlantic Monthly*, LXXXII, No. 493 (November, 1898), 592–605.


## Writings on Religion

FAIRCHILD, JAMES HARRIS. *Elements of Theology, Natural and Revealed*. Oberlin, Ohio: E. J. Goodrich, 1892.

————. *Moral Science or the Philosophy of Obligation*. New York: American Book Co., 1892.

KING, HENRY CHURCHILL. *Reconstruction in Theology*. New York: Macmillan Co., 1901.

————. *Theology and the Social Consciousness*. New York: Macmillan Co., 1902.

MILLER, PERRY, and JOHNSON, THOMAS H. (eds.). *The Puritans*. 2d ed. rev. New York: Harper and Row, 1963.

FROST, WILLIAM G. "A Word in the Pastor's Absence," *Advance*, XVI, No. 729 (September 8, 1881), 562–63.


## Writings on Reform

### Books

COMMONS, JOHN ROGERS. *Social Reform and the Church*. New York: Thomas Y. Crowell and Co., 1894.

ELLIS, JOHN MILLOTT. *Oberlin and the American Conflict*. Oberlin, Ohio: Oberlin News, 1865.

HOLBROOK, Z. SWIFT. *The Lessons of the Homestead Troubles*. Chicago: Knight, Leonard and Co., 1892.

JENKS, JEREMIAH. *The Political and Social Significance of the Life and Teachings of Jesus*. New York: Young Men's Christian Association Press, 1906.

KING, HENRY CHURCHILL. *The Moral and Religious Challenge of Our Times*. New York: Macmillan Co., 1911.

PEABODY, FRANCIS G. *Jesus Christ and the Social Question*. New York: Macmillan Co., 1900.

STRIEBY, MICHAEL E. *Oberlin and the American Missionary Association*. Cleveland: Cleveland Printing Co., 1891.

STRONG, JOSIAH. *Our Country: Its Possible Future and Its Present Crisis*. New York: Baker and Taylor, 1885.

*The Whole Story: History of the Oberlin Temperance War, 1882*. Cleveland: Leader Publishing Co., 1882.

### Articles

HOLBROOK, Z. SWIFT. "The American Republic and the Debs Insurrection (I)," *Bibliotheca Sacra*, LII (January, 1895), 135–52.

———. "The American Republic and the Debs Insurrection (II)," *Bibliotheca Sacra,* LII (April, 1895), 209–31.

———. "Christian Sociology," *Bibliotheca Sacra,* LI (October, 1894), 537–59.

WRIGHT, GEORGE FREDERICK. "Ministers and Mobs," *Bibliotheca Sacra,* XLIX (October, 1892), 676–81.

## Writings in the Social Sciences

### Books

ANDREWS, E. BENJAMIN. *Institutes of Economics.* Boston: Silver, Burdette, 1889.

BLACK, J. WILLIAM. *References on the History of Labor and Some Contemporary Labor Problems* ("Oberlin College Library Bulletin," Vol. I, No. 2). Oberlin, Ohio: Oberlin College Library, 1893.

COMMONS, JOHN ROGERS. *A Popular Bibliography of Sociology* ("Oberlin College Library Bulletin," Vol. I, No. 1). Oberlin, Ohio: Oberlin College Library, 1892.

ELY, RICHARD T. *An Introduction to Political Economy.* New York: Eaton and Mains, 1889.

———. *Problems of Today.* New York: Thomas Y. Crowell Co., 1888.

HENDERSON, CHARLES R. *An Introduction to the Study of the Dependent, Defective and Delinquent Classes.* Boston: D. C. Heath and Co., 1893.

HOLT, W. STULL (ed.). *Historical Scholarship in the United States, 1876–1901: As Revealed in the Correspondence of Herbert B. Adams.* ("The Johns Hopkins University Studies in Historical and Political Science," Vol. LVI, No. 4.) Baltimore: Johns Hopkins University Press, 1938.

### Articles

BLACK, J. WILLIAM. "Savagery and Survivals," *Popular Science Monthly,* XLV July, 1894), 388–401.

WOLFE, ALBERT B. "Social Focus of College Studies: To What Extent Do the Subjects Pursued During the Four Years of the College Course Show a Tendency Toward a Social Focus? An Investigation of the Programs of Students in One College," *Religious Education,* IX (April, 1914), 141–54.

## SECONDARY MATERIALS

## Biography

### Books

BARKER, CHARLES A. *Henry George.* New York: Oxford University Press, 1955.

KEELER, HARRIETT L. *The Life of Adelia A. Field Johnston.* Cleveland: Korner and Wood Co., 1912.

LOVE, DONALD M. *Henry Churchill King of Oberlin.* New Haven: Yale University Press, 1956.

STEUART, JUSTIN. *Wayne Wheeler, Dry Boss.* New York: Fleming H. Revell Co., 1928.

SWING, ALBERT T. *James Harris Fairchild.* New York: Fleming H. Revell Co., 1907.

A *Tribute to the Memory of John Millott Ellis, D. D.* Oberlin, Ohio: Pearce and Randolph, 1894.

### Articles

WEISENBURGER, FRANCIS P. "William Sanders Scarborough: Early Life and Years at Wilberforce," *Ohio History*, LXXI, No. 3 (October, 1962), 203–26.

————. "William Sanders Scarborough: Scholarship, the Negro, Religion, and Politics," *Ohio History*, LXXII, No. 1 (January, 1963), 25–50.

## Writings on Oberlin and Education

### Books

BAILYN, BERNARD. *Education in the Forming of American Society.* Chapel Hill: University of North Carolina Press, 1960.

BUTTS, R. FREEMAN. *The College Charts Its Course.* New York: McGraw-Hill Book Co., 1939.

FAIRCHILD, JAMES HARRIS. *Oberlin: The Colony and the College, 1833–1883.* Oberlin, Ohio: E. J. Goodrich, 1883.

FLETCHER, ROBERT SAMUEL. *A History of Oberlin College From Its Foundation Through the Civil War.* 2 vols. Oberlin, Ohio: Oberlin College, 1943.

FUESS, CLAUDE M. *Amherst, The Story of a New England College.* Boston: Little, Brown and Co., 1935.

FULLERTON, KEMPER. *Essays and Sketches.* New Haven: Yale University Press, 1938.

HAWKINS, HUGH. *Pioneer: A History of the Johns Hopkins University, 1874–1889.* Ithaca: Cornell University Press, 1960.

HOFSTADTER, RICHARD, and METZGER, WALTER P., *The Development of Academic Freedom in the United States.* (New York: Columbia University Press, 1955).

HOSFORD, FRANCES J. *Father Shipherd's Magna Charta: A Century of Coeducation in Oberlin College.* Boston: Marshall Jones Co., 1937.

JONES, LEWIS L. *Oberlin and Eastern School Life.* Warren, Ohio: Trumbull Printing Co., 1889.

KNIGHT, G. W. and COMMONS, J. R. *The History of Higher Education in Ohio.* Washington: Government Printing Office, 1891.

LEDUC, THOMAS. *Piety and Intellect at Amherst College, 1865–1912.* (No. 16 in the "Columbia Studies in American Culture"). New York: Columbia University Press, 1946.

LEONARD, DELAVAN L. *The Story of Oberlin: The Institution, the Community, the Idea, the Movement.* Boston: Pilgrim Press, 1898.

PETERSON, GEORGE E. *The New England College in the Age of the University.* Amherst, Mass.: Amherst College Press, 1964.

RUDOLPH, FREDERICK. *The American College and University: A History.* New York: Alfred A. Knopf, 1962.

————. *Mark Hopkins and the Log: Williams College, 1836–1872.* New Haven: Yale University Press, 1956.

SCHMIDT, GEORGE P. *The Old Time College President.* ("Columbia University Studies in History, Economics and Public Law," No. 317). New York: Columbia University Press, 1930.

TEWKSBURY, DONALD G. *The Founding of American Colleges and Universities Before the Civil War.* New York: Teachers College, Columbia University Press, 1932.

VEYSEY, LAURENCE R. *The Emergence of the American University.* Chicago: University of Chicago Press, 1965.

## Articles

BARNES, SHERMAN B. "Learning and Piety in Ohio Colleges, 1865–1900," *Ohio Historical Quarterly,* LXIX, No. 4 (October, 1960), 327–52.

FITCH, FLORENCE M. "President King's Training Class," *Oberlin Alumni Magazine,* IV, No. 2 (November, 1907), 38–40.

FLETCHER, ROBERT SAMUEL. "Horse and Buggy Days," *Oberlin Alumni Magazine,* XLVII, No. 1 (November, 1950), 4–5, 11.

HARTSON, LOUIS D. "The Occupations Which College Graduates Enter," *The Vocational Guidance Magazine,* VI, No. 7 (April, 1928), 297–302.

JEWETT, FRANK FANNING and JEWETT, FRANCES GULICK. "The Chemical Department of Oberlin College from 1833 to 1912," *Oberlin Alumni Magazine,* XVIII, No. 10–Supplement (July, 1922), 3–15.

RUDOLPH, FREDERICK. "Who Paid the Bills?" *Harvard Educational Review,* XXXI, No. 2 (Spring, 1961), 144–57.

WILLIAMS, SAMUEL R. "A History of Physics in Oberlin College," *Oberlin Alumni Magazine,* XI, No. 2 (November, 1914), 50–56.

# Writings on Religion

## Books

ABELL, AARON I. *The Urban Impact on American Protestantism, 1865–1900.* "Harvard Historical Studies," Vol. LIV. Cambridge: Harvard University Press, 1943.

ATKINS, GAIUS GLENN and FAGLEY, FREDERICK L. *History of American Congregationalism.* Boston: Pilgrim Press, 1942.

COLE, CHARLES C. Jr., *The Social Ideas of the Northern Evangelists, 1826–1860.* New York: Columbia University Press, 1954.

FOSTER, FRANK HUGH. *A Genetic History of the New England Theology.* Chicago: University of Chicago Press, 1907.

———. *The Modern Movement in American Theology.* New York: Fleming H. Revell Co., 1939.

HOFSTADTER, RICHARD. *Anti-Intellectualism in American Life.* New York: Alfred A. Knopf, 1963.

HOPKINS, C. HOWARD. *History of the Y.M.C.A. in North America.* New York: Association Press, 1951.

———. *The Rise of the Social Gospel in American Protestantism, 1865–1915.* "Yale Studies in Religious Education," Vol. XIV. New Haven: Yale University Press, 1940.

HORTON, WALTER M. "Systematic Theology." In *Protestant Thought in the Twentieth Century.* Edited by Arnold S. Nash. New York: Macmillan Co., 1951.

HUDSON, WINTHROP S. *American Protestantism.* Chicago: University of Chicago Press, 1961.

KINZER, DONALD L. *An Episode in Anti-Catholicism: The American Protective Association.* Seattle: University of Washington Press, 1964.

LEE, JAMES WILLIAM. "The Development of Theology at Oberlin." Unpublished Ph.D. dissertation, Drew Theological Seminary, 1952.

MAY, HENRY F. *Protestant Churches and Industrial America.* New York: Harper and Bros., 1949.

McGIFFERT, ARTHUR C. *The Rise of Modern Religious Ideas.* New York: Macmillan Co., 1915.

McLOUGHLIN, WILLIAM G. *Modern Revivalism: Charles Grandison Finney to Billy Graham.* New York: Ronald Press, 1959.

SMITH, JAMES W. and JAMISON, A. LELAND (eds.). *Religion in American Life.* Vol. I: *The Shaping of American Religion.* Princeton: Princeton University Press, 1961.

SMITH, TIMOTHY L. *Revivalism and Social Reform in Mid-Nineteenth Century America.* New York: Abingdon Press, 1957.

VISSER 'T HOOFT, W. A. *The Background of the Social Gospel in America.* Haarlem: H. D. Tjeenk Willenk and Zoon, 1928.

WALKER, WILLISTON. *A History of the Congregational Churches in the United States.* New York: Charles Scribners' Sons, 1916.

### Articles

HANDY, ROBERT T. "The Protestant Quest for a Christian America, 1830–1930," *Church History,* XXII, No. 1 (March, 1953), 8–20.

HORTON, WALTER M. "Henry Churchill King and Oberlin Liberalism," *Oberlin Today,* XVIII, No. 3 (Third Quarter, 1960), 3–22.

MEAD, SIDNEY E. "American Protestantism since the Civil War. I. From Denominationalism to Americanism," *Journal of Religion,* XXXVI, No. 1 (January, 1956), 1–16.

———. "American Protestantism since the Civil War. II. From Americanism to Christianity," *Journal of Religion,* XXXVI, No. 2 (April, 1956), 67–89.

———. "Denominationalism: The Shape of Protestantism in America," *Church History,* XXIII, No. 4 (December, 1954), 291–320.

SCHLESINGER, ARTHUR M. "A Critical Period in American Religion,1875–1900," *Proceedings of the Massachusetts Historical Society,* LXIV (June, 1932), 523–47.

### Writings on Society and Reform

DOHN, NORMAN H. "The History of the Anti-Saloon League." Unpublished Ph.D. dissertation, Dept. of History, Ohio State University, 1959.

ASBURY, HERBERT. *The Great Illusion, An Informal History of Prohibition.* Garden City, N. Y.: Doubleday and Co., 1950.

BREMNER, ROBERT H. *From the Depths: The Discovery of Poverty in the United States.* New York: New York University Press, 1956.

CHERRINGTON, ERNEST H. *Evolution of Prohibition in the United States.* Westerville, Ohio: The American Issue Publishing Co., 1920.

———. *History of the Anti-Saloon League.* Westerville, Ohio: The American Issue Publishing Co., 1913.

COMMAGER, HENRY S. *The American Mind.* New Haven: Yale University Press, 1950.

DOMBROWSKI, JAMES. *The Early Days of Christian Socialism in America*. New York: Columbia University Press, 1936.

EKIRCH, ARTHUR A. *The Idea of Progress in America, 1815–1860*. New York: Columbia University Press, 1944.

FINE, SIDNEY. *Laissez-Faire and the General Welfare State*. Ann Arbor: Ann Arbor Paperbacks, University of Michigan Press, 1964.

GABRIEL, RALPH H. *The Course of American Democratic Thought*. 2d ed. New York: Ronald Press, 1956.

HIGHAM, JOHN. *Strangers in the Land: Patterns of American Nativism, 1860–1925*. New Brunswick, N. J.: Rutgers University Press, 1955.

HOFSTADTER, RICHARD. *The Age of Reform*. New York: Alfred A. Knopf, 1955.

———. *Social Darwinism in American Thought*. 2d ed. revised. Boston: Beacon Press, 1955.

KROUT, JOHN A. *The Origins of Prohibition*. New York: Alfred A. Knopf, 1925.

MAY, HENRY F. *The End of American Innocence*. New York: Alfred A. Knopf, 1959.

MOWRY, GEORGE E. *The Era of Theodore Roosevelt*. New York: Harper, 1958.

ODEGARD, PETER H. *Pressure Politics: The Story of the Anti-Saloon League*. New York: Columbia University Press, 1928.

PERSONS, STOW. *American Minds; A History of Ideas*. New York: Henry Holt and Co., 1958.

SINCLAIR, ANDREW. *Prohibition: The Era of Excess*. Boston: Little, Brown and Co., 1962.

TIMBERLAKE, JAMES H. *Prohibition and the Progressive Movement, 1900–1920*. Cambridge: Harvard University Press, 1963.

## Writings on the Social Sciences

### Books

BERNARD, L. L. and BERNARD, JESSIE. *Origins of American Sociology*. New York: Thomas Y. Crowell Co., 1943.

DORFMAN, JOSEPH. *The Economic Mind in American Civilization, 1606–1865*. 2 vols. New York: Viking Press, 1946.

———. *The Economic Mind in American Civilization*. Vol. III: *1865–1918*. New York: Viking Press, 1949.

———. *The Economic Mind in American Civilization*. Vols. IV and V: *1918–1933*. New York: Viking Press, 1959.

HADDOW, ANNA. *Political Science in American Colleges and Universities, 1636–1900*. New York: C. Appleton-Century Co., 1939.

HERBST, JURGEN. *The German Historical School in American Scholarship*. Ithaca, N. Y.: Cornell University Press, 1965.

O'CONNOR, MICHAEL J. L. *Origins of Academic Economics in the United States*. New York: Columbia University Press, 1944.

### Articles

BRYSON, GLADYS. "The Comparable Interests of the Old Moral Philosophy and the Modern Social Sciences," *Social Forces*, XI, No. 1 (October, 1932), 26–36.

———. "The Emergence of the Social Sciences from Moral Philosphy," *International Journal of Ethics*, XLII, No. 3 (April, 1932), 304–323.

———. "Sociology Considered as Moral Philosophy," *Sociological Review,* XXIV, No. 1 (January, 1932), 26–36.

FLETCHER, ROBERT SAMUEL. "History in Oberlin," *Oberlin Alumni Magazine,* XLVIII, No. 1 (November, 1951), 4, 15.

SMALL, ALBION. "Fifty Years of Sociology in the United States (1865–1915)," *American Journal of Sociology,* XXI, No. 6 (May, 1916), 721–864.


*Writings on State and Local History*


GALBREATH, CHARLES B. *History of Ohio,* 5 vols. Chicago: American Historical Society, Inc., 1925.

JORDAN, PHILIP D. *Ohio Comes of Age, 1873–1900.* Vol. V of *The History of the State of Ohio.* Edited by Carl Wittke. Columbus: Ohio State Archaeological and Historical Society, 1943.

ROSEBOOM, EUGENE H. and WEISENBURGER, FRANCIS P. *A History of Ohio.* Columbus: Ohio State Archaeological and Historical Society, 1953.

WRIGHT, GEORGE FREDERICK (ed). *A Standard History of Lorain County Ohio.* Chicago: Lewis Publishing Co., 1916.

# INDEX